SURVIVING THE IRON AGE

Contents

QUOTATIONS FROM CLASSICAL WRITERS ARE TAKEN FROM:

Athenaeus, *Deipnosophistae*, tr. C.B. Gulick (Harvard University Press, Harvard, 1928)
Caesar, Julius, *Gallic War*, tr. H. Edwards (Harvard University Press, Harvard, 1917)
Dio, Cassius, *Roman History*, tr. E. Cary (Harvard University Press, Harvard, 1914)
Siculus, Diodorus, *Historical Library*, tr. C.H. Oldfather (Harvard University Press, Harvard, 1933)
Mann, J.C. and Penman, R.G. (ed.), *Literary Sources for Roman Britain*, LACTOR 11 (2nd ed.), (LACT Publications, Harrow, 1985)
Polybius, *The Histories*, tr. W.R. Paton (Harvard University Press, Harvard, 1922)
Strabo, *Geography*, tr. H.L. Jones (Harvard University Press, Harvard, 1917)
Tacitus, *Annuls*, tr. J. Jackson (Harvard University Press, Harvard, 1931)

Acknowledgements

My thanks go first of all to the seventeen volunteers who bravely put themselves forward for this living history project. Without their co-operation and commitment, neither the television series nor the book would have been possible.

We relied on the advice of many experts in their field, including Professor Barry Cunliffe, Dr Harold Mytum, Dr Martin Elphick, Henrietta Smethurst, Peter and Susan Crewe, the Cantiaci living history group and in particular Phil Bennett, manager at Castell Henllys, whose archaeological advice was invaluable.

Many people in west Pembrokeshire and further afield generously gave us their support during the project. It is impossible to list them all, but many thanks are due to Judy and Rhidian Lewis and Ian and Margaret Metcalf for their support with the animals, and to Berrian Lewis, Bob Shaw, John Reading, Christopher and Anna Nickson, David Redpath, John Denley, Diane John and Maggie Smith. My thanks also go to the staff at Castell Henllys, and in particular to Lloyd George, John McDermot, Rhonwen Owen, Pat Haynes, Karen Everson, Liz Moore, Liz Rooney, Nicola Hancox and Stuart Wilkinson.

There were many people at BBC Bristol involved with the production of the television series whom I would like to thank, including the directors Martin Pailthorpe and Emma Wooster, producer Kath Moore, Tiggi Trethowan, Danny Cane, Jill Wellington, David Postlethwaite, Rob Llewellyn, Darren Tate, Rick Holbrook, Harmeet Sehambi, Deirdre Laister, Sue Oakey, Marlon Griffin, Ben Lockwood and finally, executive producers Andy Batten-Foster and Tessa Finch.

My thanks also go to Lucy Lamble and Dudley Curtis at BBC Online for their work on the website, and to Sally Potter, Erica Jeal and Linda Blakemore at BBC Worldwide who performed their own sort of magic on my manuscript.

My final thanks go to my wife and children, for patiently putting up with me being away for long periods and for hogging the best computer in the house when I am back.

◁ The Snettisham 'Great Torc', dating from around 70 BC, has a diameter of 199mm (8in) and is arguably the finest of its kind yet found in Britain. The hoop is made from eight spiral strands, with each strand made from eight wires twisted to form a hollow tube.

▽ Maiden Castle, one of the biggest and most elaborate hillforts in Britain. The multiple ramparts and ditches enclose an area of 19 hectares (47 acres).

Introduction

THE CELTIC IRON AGE IS OFTEN CONSIDERED TO BE the poor cousin of British history, overshadowed by the later Roman occupation of our islands. Yet this period is amongst the greatest and most successful of the early European cultures. For hundreds of years Celtic language, culture and art influenced most of the European continent, from the Iberian peninsular in the south to France and Germany in the north, and from the Atlantic coast of Ireland as far east as the Balkans and even Turkey.

The early Celts were portrayed by the Greek and Roman historians as defiant, dangerous and unpredictable. These writers were fascinated by the bizarre and grotesque elements of Celtic life – ritual human sacrifice, headhunting, the alleged promiscuity of their women and the 'magical rites' of their druid priests. Perhaps most enduring of all is their reputation for setting alight giant figures built from wicker and straw, which contained living human beings and animals, as offerings to their gods.

However, modern archaeologists now see the Celts as a sophisticated group of societies which experienced great technological and social change. They mastered the production of iron, and their culture became more complex and gave rise to a warrior aristocracy. This in turn laid the foundation of the British feudal system. The Celts were a tribal people, hierarchical and agricultural, with deeply held superstitions and religious beliefs rooted in the natural world. They were also a very creative society and their craftsmen produced a high quality, abstract art of curvilinear design, which is very different from the Classical and Renaissance traditions. Their art might appear strange and mysterious to our eyes, yet it defines their civilization and has rightly been described as one of the greatest glories of prehistoric Europe.

The Greek politician Polybius wrote of the Celts of northern Italy that 'their lives were very simple, and they had no knowledge whatsoever of any art or science.' He could not have been further from the truth.

▷ The twenty-first century was never far away: the volunteers wave goodbye to the helicopter in early October after a morning filming the aerials for the series.

This book is intended to complement a BBC television series in which seventeen people were taken back in time to experience life as we think it might have been in Celtic Britain. These people, including three children, bravely volunteered to spend nearly seven weeks living in an Iron Age hillfort in west Wales, in conditions which sometimes resembled penal servitude of the most punishing kind.

This was an ambitious experiment in 'living history', but there was never any intention to try to understand how people lived during the Iron Age. Our volunteers were from the twenty-first century and nothing could eradicate their accumulated knowledge of past history and present experience. It was not for them to try to second-guess how the Iron Age people lived; those prehistoric people were influenced by pagan beliefs and a profound suspicion of the outside world which we could never hope to fully understand, let alone replicate.

Our objective was much more straightforward: it was to see if a group of people from the modern world could organize themselves in an alien, prehistoric environment. How would they manage to live in the harsh conditions which were the regular day-to-day experience for ancient Celts? How would they cope with the relentless menial tasks which occupied much of the day for prehistoric people? What would it feel like to wear the clothing of early Britons? Would they remain healthy on a diet of spelt wheat, meat and kale? Could they make candles and soap, kill a chicken, produce charcoal and, perhaps most difficult of all, would they succeed in mastering the 'magical' art of smelting iron from ore?

The results of the experiment were surprising – both for the BBC production team and for the volunteers. Not everybody stayed the course, but those who did learnt enormous respect for the skills of the Iron Age people, not to mention a profound understanding of the relentless, daily grind of hard labour which was the reality of life in Celtic Britain. They also learnt much about themselves as individuals, as well as about their place in the twenty-first century.

With only a few exceptions, I have concentrated throughout this book on Celtic Britain, but the reading list at the back will help direct readers to other books which cover Iron Age life in continental Europe. I also hope that the second appendix, which lists some of the Iron Age reconstructed sites in Britain, will encourage readers to visit a roundhouse for themselves and to try to visualize what life must have been like in Britain over two thousand years ago.

It has only been possible to scratch the surface of the subject in a book such as this. I have assumed that most readers come to the subject with only a vague idea of

what life was like in pre-Roman Britain. Therefore, after introducing the project and the volunteers themselves, I have given a brief sketch, in Chapter 3, of what life might have been like 'before iron', in order to prepare the ground for understanding life in Iron Age Britain.

I have developed great respect for the weeks of back-breaking labour which archaeologists spend on site and often many more weeks of lengthy analysis once back at base. I am also aware of the many debates raging within archaeology about the period of the Celts. Long may this be the case, for out of debate grows a greater understanding of our history. But this book is an introduction to the period for the general reader and is not intended for the expert, so I make no apology for skirting some of the more contentious issues, nor for simplifying some of the complexities of the subject. However, my biggest concern is that mistakes and errors can always creep into any text. If this is so, then the responsibility is mine alone.

Peter Firstbrook
November AD 2000, London

◁ The aerodynamic shape of an Iron Age roundhouse can withstand winds in excess of 100 mph.

▽ The reconstructed roundhouses at Castell Henllys have been built directly on the foundations of original Iron Age buildings; it is the only site of its kind in Britain.

1
The Fort on the Hill

THE OLD MAN LAY MOTIONLESS IN HIS BED, eyes tightly closed, trying to identify the sounds and smells of early morning. It was a game he liked to play every morning before he rose for the day. He had been on fire duty during the night and he could smell the smoke from the oak he had put on the fire a couple of hours ago. He liked the smell of oak. It was richer, somehow stronger than beech or ash, but not as sweet as apple.

Inside the roundhouse, he could hear the gentle breathing of his wife lying next to him. Nearby, another couple turned restlessly, their hay mattress rustling under the weight of their bodies. The young boy coughed in his sleep. Outside, the birds had already begun their dawn chorus. The old man could recognize the sounds of the different birds, but there was a new song now from the small birds who had settled in the trees just a few days before. He knew that soon they would fly off in the direction of the midday sun to another land, only to return the following spring. It was like this every year. The birds always left before his people celebrated Samhain, always before the winter storms brought the chill winds.

The old man opened his eyes slowly. The milky-blue light of dawn was already beginning to seep under the eaves of the roundhouse. He could see the outline of the cauldron hanging over the fire and the benches clustered around the hearth. It was already daybreak, time to rise. He tried to ease himself from his bed so as not to disturb his wife, but the wattle base cracked and rustled like a badger walking through the undergrowth. His wife rolled away from him, oblivious to the noise.

Carefully skirting the earthen hearth, he gently stepped over the heavy quern-stones lying to one side. The womenfolk needed them close to the doorway to use every minute of daylight to grind their corn, and often he had stubbed his toe on the heavy stone blocks. But not this time. He pulled open the wattle door and stooped under the heavy wooden lintel.

▽ Castell Henllys is one of several Iron Age sites located in the beautiful North Pembrokeshire Coast National Park.

Outside it was a clear morning. The low sun made him screw up his eyes after the gloom of the roundhouse; brightness pierced the tree canopy as if burnishing the autumn-tinged oak leaves. A red flash to his left caught his eye as he glimpsed a vixen before she darted nervously behind the palisade. Perhaps somebody had left some bones out last night, or perhaps the fox was nosing hopefully around the chicken house.

He enjoyed the early mornings. Nobody else was yet up and he still had the hillfort to himself. As he stretched his back and rubbed his aching muscles, he looked out across the valley to the Preseli hills beyond, no more than a two-hour walk away. The rolling hills stretched to the east as far as the eye could see, and round to the west, where they seemed to sink down below the ocean. The Preselis were the source of the bluestone used to construct the inner circle at Stonehenge countless generations before and the distant hills still retained an aura of mystery and magic. And there, in the direction where the sun set over the mountains, was Carningli, another hillfort built on a towering rocky summit, which dominated the surrounding area.

The view across the Nevern valley was a familiar sight to many thousands of Iron Age Celts who lived in the hillfort at Castell Henllys over a period of six or seven hundred years. An old man must have stood on that very spot a million times or more looking south across the rolling hills, wondering what the day would bring. But in a fascinating journey into living history, that autumn morning also became familiar to a group of seventeen volunteers drafted in from the twenty-first century to live in Iron Age conditions for a period of almost two months. It was an experience which created and cemented friendships but also brought

△ The autumn of 2000 was the wettest since rainfall records were first kept in 1727. Nineteen inches of rain fell in three months, 86 per cent above the long-term average.

conflict and tears. A few of the volunteers would leave before the end, but most stayed the course to complete an experience which money could not buy – an opportunity to go back 2,500 years to discover how people from the modern world would cope with Iron Age life.

The original proposal for BBC1 was to make a series of programmes, each covering a different period of British history. During the late 1970s, the BBC in Bristol had made a remarkable series in which fifteen people, including three young children, had spent thirteen months living in Iron Age conditions. The series, called *Living in the Past*, was produced by John Percival and was shown on BBC2 to critical acclaim. The BBC therefore decided that this new experiment in 'experiential history' should start by repeating the Iron Age period. Not only is this a fascinating period of British history, but there would be the additional interest of comparing the experiences of the volunteers in the late 1970s with those of the people selected for the new project.

Once the decision was taken to make the new series, it was decided that the filming could not wait until the spring of 2001, but had to be shot by the autumn of

2000. The summer of 2000 therefore began with frenetic activity. A suitable existing site had to be found because there was no time to build a new settlement as for the previous series. Even more difficult was finding a suitably skilled and enthusiastic group of people who would be able to give up seven weeks at short notice and subject themselves to the challenge of living in the Iron Age – and the notoriety that inevitably comes from participating in these television programmes.

In many ways, finding a suitable site was a straightforward research effort. In the 1970s series, the producer wanted to start with a greenfield site and have his volunteers build a roundhouse and associated buildings from scratch. This construction phase was all part of the original project, which lasted for over a year. For the new series, we needed to find a pre-existing location. The choice was between a typical lowland farmstead and living in grander style in an Iron Age hillfort, which would have been home to a local chieftain and his extended family. Both the farmstead and the hillfort would have had similar circular buildings, but the type of people and the purpose of the settlement would have been very different.

The farmstead was the basic settlement in Iron Age Britain, populated by a family of freemen. The farm might include an extended family of three or even four generations, all descended from a common great-grandfather. These small farming settlements would have been scattered throughout Britain during the Iron Age and in many cases only a mile or two would separate neighbours. The land around their settlement would be communally owned by the family, who would pay a tax or tithe to the local chieftain or to one or more of the local warrior nobles.

A typical farming settlement comprised one or more roundhouses inside a compound, which was ringed by a ditch and a low bank topped with a wooden perimeter fence. The buildings would be made from timber, wattle, daub and thatch, and would offer communal living and sleeping areas with little privacy. Within the compound, there would also be other smaller structures such as a granary, animal enclosures, haystacks and storage pits. The perimeter fence would keep livestock and children in and scavenging and dangerous animals out, but it would not have had any significant defensive purpose. These farming people relied on the protective umbrella offered by the local chieftain and warrior nobles and not on any inherent defensive skills or structures of their own.

The alternative option was to base the television series in an Iron Age hillfort, which would have been a bigger settlement with many more dwellings than a farmstead. It would, by definition, also have been built on a hill or headland. Iron Age hillforts such as Maiden Castle in Dorset, Cadbury Castle in Somerset and Danebury in Hampshire are some of the most impressive ancient monuments in the country and in those areas they tower above today's skyline as much as they did when they were built, over two thousand years ago.

Hillforts are large, defended enclosures, often constructed with several rows of fortifications comprising ditches and banks, topped with a wooden fence. Over the centuries, hillforts probably had several functions: as their name implies, they were certainly fortified sites, but at times they also formed peaceful settlements and on other occasions they were probably places for social gatherings or annual fairs.

It is likely that a hillfort was usually inhabited by a chieftain or local king and several warrior nobles, together with their extended families and a retinue of unfree clients and slaves. Skilled craftsmen might also have lived there, but farmers and freemen would have lived in farmsteads in the surrounding area. In the case of

HILLFORTS IN SOUTHERN BRITAIN

Some of the best-researched sites are in southern Britain, when the first Iron Age hillforts were built in around 800 to 600 BC. This early stage of building produced a few large hillforts, widely dispersed throughout the region. Sites such as Bindon Hill near Lulworth in Dorset were very large indeed and covered many hectares. Other hillforts built during this period include Bathampton Down near Bath, Hartington Beacon in Sussex, Winklebury near Basingstoke and Balkesbury in Hampshire.

During the sixth century BC, there was a spate of building in southern Britain and strongly defended forts grew up throughout the region. These hillforts were smaller, typically about 5 hectares (12 acres). Danebury was built during this period and is typical of many of the hillforts built during the century. The site was enclosed by a single rampart and ditch and a roadway ran through the centre connecting two entrances. There were probably secondary tracks running off connecting roundhouses, granaries and storage pits. The area to the north of the road was given over to four-post granaries, soon replaced by densely packed storage pits. This sector might have been used for storing communal supplies of surplus grain from farmsteads outside the hillfort.

It seems likely that this spate of fort building in the sixth century BC preceded a period of social and political change in southern Britain, which occurred between 600 and 350 BC. This might have been a time of periodic conflict and instability with tribes competing for supremacy in the region and these hillforts being built to assert their power and justify their authority.

▷ The excavated parts of Danebury hillfort show the density of
archaeological features (mainly storage pits and post holes) and
the pattern of roadways.

▽ A close-up of the south-western part of the hillfort gives a
good indication of the complexity of an Iron Age site.

0   150 yards

0   150 metres

N

0   50 yards

0   50 metres

Danebury, it has been estimated that between 200 and 350 people might have lived
in the fort. Nobles and their families might also have resided in some of the smaller,
satellite hillforts in the region, also supported by nearby farms. Some hillforts might
not have been settled permanently at all, but used for temporary occupation
during social gatherings such as an annual fair, or at times of religious festivals.

The search for a suitable location for filming took several weeks and a number of
sites around southern Britain were examined, mostly single roundhouses typical
of an Iron Age farmstead (see Appendix 2, page 184). However, one site stood out
from the rest. It was a small hillfort with four roundhouses, a four-post granary
and a chicken house. What made this particular site unique was that the recon-

▽ When Castell Henllys hillfort was occupied during the
Iron Age, the site would have been kept clear of trees to give
look-outs a clear view of the surrounding area.

structed buildings were situated *directly* on the site of an original Celtic hillfort which had been inhabited for over 600 years. The site was first excavated in 1981 and the post-holes from the original buildings had been used – hole matching hole – to erect new buildings on the site. Although only four houses had been built on the hillfort, which originally might have contained ten or twelve, the new roundhouses were as authentic as possible. Their size and shape were the same as the original Iron Age buildings and even the doorways faced in the same direction as they had more than two thousand years previously.

The hillfort was called Castell Henllys and was owned by the North Pembroke-shire Coast National Park in west Wales. The site was open to the public during the summer months and was not only an important tourist attraction in the region, but was also used as an educational centre for the schoolchildren of Wales.

Whilst the site was ideal for the purposes of filming, it was obvious from the outset that filming and visitors would not mix. But would the National Park agree to close the site for a period of seven weeks in the autumn?

Meanwhile, the search began for a group of volunteers to live on the site. For the 1970s series, the BBC simply advertised in *The Times* for anyone who was interested and received nearly 2000 enquiries. Attracting volunteers twenty-five years later was a little more complicated. It would have taken several weeks to process the large number of applicants if we repeated a nationwide advertisement, and time was already beginning to run out if filming was to start in September. Instead, a more focused approach was adopted and the production team decided on the ages and backgrounds of the people required to make up the group. These people were then targeted through mailshots and websites.

Unlike the 1970s project which contained couples all in their late twenties, the new series would have a much more diverse range of ages, from young children through to older couples, making the group more representative of a true Iron Age community. We also decided on the skills and experience which would help these people through their time in the Iron Age, and targeted people with the relevant abilities. For example, metalworking was a fundamental skill in the Iron Age, so over 400 letters were written to blacksmiths across the country. Likewise, experience with livestock and growing one's own food would be useful skills, as would wood-land management and camping experience. We wrote to supply agencies asking for teachers who would be able to maintain the education of the children on site, and we approached hospitals and medical organizations for suitably qualified volun-teers to join the team, including people with knowledge of herbal medicine. Ritual and religion were also an important part of Celtic life, so we contacted druidic groups in the search for somebody with knowledge of traditional pagan beliefs.

For several weeks, researchers monitored telephone calls and e-mails as hundreds of people contacted us for more information. It was a delicate balancing act as we tried to select people of different ages, including couples with children, who could offer a diversity of skills to the group. We also wanted to link this new series to the original one, so we contacted all the volunteers from the 1970s project to invite their children, now in their late teens and early twenties, to take part in the new series.

By July 2000, an agreement had been reached with the National Park to have exclusive access to the Castell Henllys hillfort for a period of seven weeks, beginning on 16 September. This allowed the Park to make the most of the summer period, but allowed the BBC to start filming in late summer. The plan was for the volunteers to move in on Sunday 17 September and stay until Wednesday 1 November. This would enable the group to celebrate Samhain on 31 October – the most important festival in the calendar of the early Celts (see Chapter 11). Samhain (pronounced *Sam-hane* by archaeologists and *Sow-hane* by historians and modern druids) marks the end of the Celtic year, and this seemed an appropriate time to complete the filming. It is a dark and foreboding festival when the early Celts believed that long dead ancestors could return to commune with the living.

Meanwhile, the long process of carefully selecting the applicants for the project continued. From the outset, we made the 'rules of the game' clear to the prospective volunteers. The BBC takes on a moral and legal responsibility when people become involved in a filming project, so living in *totally* authentic Iron Age conditions was never an option. Health and safety had to be priorities at all times and would not be compromised for the sake of the filming. So concessions had to be made to the modern world, but they were strictly limited.

First, all volunteers were asked to undergo a full medical examination. They were to be provided with clean, fresh drinking water and a mains tap was located at the bottom of the site close to the river, where the original Iron Age inhabitants obtained their own water supply. Each individual could also continue taking any medication they might require, subject to the approval of their GP or consultant. Finally, the women could continue to use their chosen form of contraception. With these three exceptions – water, medication and contraception – the group were expected to live like early Britons, wearing the same clothes and finding natural, primitive alternatives for soap, detergents, toothpaste, and so on.

There was one big outstanding issue which was constantly debated by the production team and which became known at the 'T' issue; should the women be allowed access to tampons and sanitary towels? Working on the assumption that it is always easier to give concessions than to reclaim them, the firm line taken at the outset was that the women would have to find natural solutions to cope with menstruation. The question was discussed at an early stage with the prospective female volunteers and, to their eternal credit, all of the chosen group agreed in principle to abide by the 'no tampon' rule. However, as the date of filming grew closer, so the hard line amongst the production team began to weaken. Nobody knows what Iron Age women did about their monthly periods, but in primitive

▽ The interior of the chieftain's roundhouse, home to the Rickards and the Phillips for seven weeks. The roundhouse is dominated by a central fire, surrounded by wooden benches. The sleeping cubicles can be seen in the background.

societies today it is common for menstruating women to spend their time together in isolation in a hut. Clearly this was not an option for our nouveau Iron Age women, who had a scant seven weeks living on the site. In the end, the 'no tampon' rule was relaxed, despite the fact that the woman volunteers had already agreed to do without.

Rules also applied to the production team and film crews whenever they were working at the hillfort. Wristwatches had to be removed or kept covered, and the date and time were not to be discussed in front of the volunteers. No food or drink was to be consumed in their vicinity and nobody was to discuss the news, the weather or any other contemporary issue within earshot of the Iron Age people. Inevitably, these rules were broken; the volunteers developed remarkable hearing at times, risked a strained neck as they tried to read a partially exposed wristwatch upside-down, and newspapers and chocolate bars mysteriously disappeared from the back of the producer's car on occasion!

Once the volunteers had been selected and had passed their medical examination, they were sent written details of what to expect on arrival at the hillfort – and what would be expected of them in return. They would live in conditions similar to those experienced by late-Iron Age Britons, in around 300 BC, a period when the Iron Age had developed to its full potential and diversity but before the early Britons were influenced by the Romans. It was stressed again that we did not expect the volunteers to live and behave as Iron Age people. They were from the twenty-first century and all that could be asked of them was to live for nearly seven weeks under Iron Age conditions and to react and respond as people from our modern world to the opportunities and limitations that the historical period offered.

▽ The Iron Age volunteers were supplied with egg-laying chickens. Unfortunately, they could not always find where the eggs were laid!

Unlike the original series, in which the volunteers worked for three months to build their own round-house and make their own clothing, our volunteers would move into an established settlement, with all four roundhouses fully equipped with beds, mattresses and blankets (see Appendix 1, page 182, for a full list). They would have fires, ovens and utensils with which to cook, and tools and equipment to work as the early Britons did at weaving, metalworking, animal husbandry, woodland management and pottery. These tasks became known as 'time challenges' and were an essential part of the project – the idea was not simply to survive, but to be creative and try to master Iron Age skills and expertise to the best of the volunteers' ability. The time challenges were printed on paper scrolls and left in the cleft of a tree for the chieftain to collect. They gave the Iron-Agers sufficient information to attempt to master the relevant task. Where necessary, the volunteers were also given expert advice and guidance, especially where health and safety issues were involved.

△ Gordon and Guy were expected to give early warning of any foxes on the prowl, and Diamond and Jock kept the volunteers well-supplied with goat's milk.

They were also told that when they arrived on site, there would be enough ready-prepared food for them to survive on for several days. But during those first few days they would have to master basic skills such as grinding corn, cooking over open fires and butchering their livestock in order to maintain their food supply. They would be provided with a wide variety of animals, including cows, pigs, sheep, goats, geese and chickens, which would provide them with milk, cheese, eggs and meat.

There was one final request made of them. The Iron Age Britons knew nothing of democracy. They were ruled under the absolute authority of their chieftain, which they either accepted or challenged. We wanted our volunteers to live under similar rules and we asked them to elect their own chieftain on their first afternoon.

There was also a practical reason for this request, for somebody needed to be a spokesperson and a main point of contact with the BBC. The chieftain could be male or female, young or old, but once elected, the group was expected to accede to his or her authority until the end of the project – or select a replacement.

◁◁ Helen and Martin Elphick (parents of Jody and Mark) during their own Iron Age experience in the late 1970s.
◁ Jill Granger and Peter Little (Tom's parents) also spent a year living in the Iron Age as part of the original BBC series.
▽ The volunteers in September 2000, about to enter the Iron Age. The eighteenth member of the group is Gwin, a Scottish Deerhound.

2

The New Iron-Agers

SEVERAL HUNDRED PEOPLE SHOWED AN INTEREST in joining the Iron Age project and it was a lengthy process filtering potential volunteers. Many discounted themselves once they knew that they would have to be there for nearly seven weeks. Others showed initial interest but gradually got cold feet. Even so, it would have been possible to fill the hillfort several times over with people who were keen to join. In the end, an attempt was made to select a compatible group of people with diverse but complementary skills. Most important of all, the one thing they all had in common was a passion and enthusiasm for living in Iron Age conditions, albeit for very different reasons.

Mark and Jody Elphick, together with Tom Little, were invited to join the series because their parents had been involved in the original Iron Age project twenty-three years previously. Most of the 'Iron Age' families had stayed in touch over the years and the children who were born after the original television series was made were brought up almost like cousins, seeing each other once or twice a year. The 'Iron Age children', as they came to be known, had often talked of repeating the experiment which had become such a big part of their parents' lives. At the time of the new series, most of them were either still at school, travelling or starting their careers. So in the event, only Mark, Jody and Tom, together with his girlfriend Ceris Williams, were free to join the project.

Jody Elphick was born just two years after her parents finished their Iron Age experience and she celebrated her twenty-first birthday during her own Iron Age project. When she heard about the new television series, she was coming

Jody Elphick (20)

Born 1979 in Oxford. Celebrated her twenty-first birthday during the project. Daughter of Martin and Helen Elphick, original Iron Age volunteers during the 1970s. Currently studying Philosophy and English at Sussex University. Interested in the arts, painting, drawing, pottery, reading and walking, but claims to spend most of her time in Brighton eating, drinking and clubbing.

to the end of her second year at university. 'I was really surprised when my brother rang me up in Brighton and said we'd had this phone call and possibly it was going to happen. I was just so shocked. I couldn't believe it. I thought he was playing a joke on me. I suppose when I realized that it was really going to happen, I got really excited. We've always wanted to do it. All the kids have always nagged at mums and dads and said couldn't we do a children's Iron Age thing, ever since we were little.'

Jody could not get permission to start her final year at university late, so she decided to take a year's break from her studies so that she could volunteer for the Iron Age series. After her A-levels, she had spent a month on an expedition to Peru, so she felt that she had some experience living within a small group of people under difficult conditions.

Mark Elphick (18)

Born 1981 in Oxford. Son of Martin and Helen Elphick. Completed his A levels in June 2000 in Art, Biology and Geography and plans to travel around Europe with friends and then across Africa with his father during his gap year. Intends to read Human Geography at university. Interests include football, fencing and playing the guitar.

Mark Elphick is two years younger than his sister Jody and was about to take a gap year after finishing his A levels when he heard about the new television series, so the chance to live in the Iron Age fitted perfectly with his plans. Mark and his sister had spent most of their lives on their parents' smallholding in Garsington near Oxford and they were accustomed to having animals around, including sheep, pigs, chickens and ducks. Their father Martin also maintained a sizeable vegetable patch, so both Mark and Jody felt reasonably prepared for self-sufficiency. Despite having grown up knowing about his parents' experience, Mark still harboured misgivings about the opportunity. 'Obviously I've got all these preconceptions and I've seen the edited videos of what they did. But there's a lot of it that we didn't see and that Mum and Dad probably haven't told us about. So I'm sure there'll be a lot of harsh reality when I actually get out and have to work all day, and quite a bit of physical labour.'

Tom Little, the third of the 'Iron Age children', was brought up near Telford. Like Jody and Mark, he lives in the country and enjoys open-air pursuits, including skiing, canoeing, cycling and climbing. Like Mark Elphick, Tom was planning to take a gap year from his studies, so he too leapt at the chance to experience life in the Iron Age. Tom had worked as a kitchen porter and chef, so it is not surprising that food was high on his list of concerns. 'One thing that I'm a bit worried about is the food, 'cos if it's just bread and that sort of thing, it's going to get fairly boring pretty quickly. In a way, food is quite important, though I'll eat pretty much what's put in front of me. But I prefer to have a relatively varied diet, rather than just bread … I wouldn't be too sure about killing animals … but then I suppose I'd have to do it, or eat bread!'

Tom also asked if his eighteen-year-old girlfriend Ceris Williams could join the project. Ceris had just finished her A levels in Art, Sculpture, English Literature and Psychology. Apart from her obvious artistic talents, she also had valuable countryside skills, taught to her by her father. 'I was really enthusiastic about living in the Iron Age because Jill [Tom's mother] had always spoken about it and told me all the stories from when they did it. It sounded great, but from what Jill says, it's quite hard work when you're there. Ever since I was young, my dad and I have gone out rabbiting and things and I used to go to the range with him and do a lot of shooting … we've also done a lot of archery together, so I've always been outdoors and in the woods.'

There were two groups of parents on the project, David and Anne Rickard with their son Christopher, and Jonathan ('Bill') and Yasmin Billinghurst with their two children Laszlo and Rosie. David and Anne live in a small village in Dorset where they describe themselves as living the 'good life', with obvious reference to the BBC television series of the same name. David is an environmental consultant and a decade ago they decided to 'reclaim our own time and lives'

Tom Little (19)
Born 1980 in Shrewsbury. His parents Peter Little and Jill Granger took part in the 1970s Iron Age experiment. He studied Photography after leaving school before taking a gap year which has allowed him to join the Iron Age project. He is interested in music, art, reading and photography, and has worked as a kitchen porter and a chef.

Ceris Williams (18)
Born 1982 in Cannock. Girlfriend of Tom Little. She has recently completed her A levels, and was awarded a grade A in Sculpture. Currently taking a gap year before going on to study Art. Her interests include playing and teaching the flute, art and sculpture, and outdoor pursuits including walking, camping, trapping and fishing – all taught to her by her father.

and live a more ecologically sound existence in the country. They refer to their large garden as a 'micro-holding' where they grow organic vegetables and fruit and keep chickens. Occasionally they rear orphan lambs 'for the freezer' and they have also kept pigs. They regularly gather wild food from the hedgerows, and nettle soup and elderflower fritters are their specialities. David obviously thought this was a golden opportunity to put their experience into practice. 'The appeal of the project is that of doing something completely different. This opportunity won't come past again –

Anne Rickard (51)

Born 1949 in Sidcup, Kent. Married David Rickard in 1987. Mother of Christopher. Worked as a secretary before moving to their present 'micro-holding' in April 1990. Enjoys travelling. An accomplished singer, she performs with an all-female trio called 'Dangerous Curves' singing in close harmony 'with a leaning towards comedy'.

David Rickard (55)

Born 1945 in Liverpool but grew up in London. Married to Anne and father of Christopher. A consultant ecologist with long experience in the water industry. 'Side-shifted' to Dorset in 1990. Like his wife, an accomplished musician – he performs in a duo called 'String Whistle', playing folk, blues, popular music and his own compositions.

Christopher Rickard (12)

Born 1988 in Dartford, Kent and moved to Dorset at the age of one. Son of David and Anne. Educated at home, which he prefers, 'because I can choose what I want to do and I have more time to play'. Likes history, cycling, cricket and tennis. Enjoys inventing things, digging for archaeological remains, climbing trees and looking for interesting things in the river.

an opportunity perhaps to put into action thoughts that I've had. We tend to live quite close to the land, we're into organic gardening and permaculture, and we've had animals. We sort of associate ourselves with the 'good life', although obviously we're not totally reliant on it. This will be a chance to see whether in fact we're as good at being dependent on nature as perhaps we think we are. So I think it'll be very interesting to see how we do cope!'

Anne Rickard always had high hopes for life in the Iron Age, although she began to fret about some of the details. 'I'm not sure what the facilities will be like and that's one thing that's been on my mind … especially how we girls are going to cope, because I've been told there'll be no knickers, so I really don't know what we're going to do!' Apart from their interest in living ecologically, David and Anne were also keen to join the project because their son Christopher was fascinated by Iron Age history. Christopher was being educated at home by his parents and Anne first heard about the television series on a home-educators' e-mail chat line. 'I couldn't just press that delete button and get rid of it. I had to go through with it. I thought, well let's just see what happens. I'm sure we won't get chosen, but at least I won't have to feel guilty for not having tried. So I got on the phone … and then the rest of it's living history. Here we are … and my son's so excited!'

Christopher Rickard was twelve when his family was invited to join the Iron Age project. Ever since Christopher moved to Dorset at the age of one, the Iron Age has surrounded him. Their house lies within sight of Maiden Castle, Britain's biggest and most impressive Iron Age hillfort. And down the road there is a reconstructed Iron Age farmstead at Bradford Peverell, so this might have had something to do with his fascination with the period. Whatever the reason, he takes at least partial responsibility for getting his parents involved in the project. 'When I was about five or six, I asked

my Mum if I could live as a Celtic boy and Mum phoned Bradford Peverell up the road and said, "Can Chris come along and have a day or two with you?" He says, "I'm sorry, he's too young." A few years later, this thing comes along and she goes, "Oh, I'll phone up." So she phones up and we get very interested. And now we know we're doing it, so it's Mum's fault as well, I'd say!'

Bill and Yasmin Billing-hurst were the other parents with children in the group, Laszlo aged five and Rosie aged four. They had different motivations from the Rickards for joining the project. Yasmin had been restless and was looking for something new to do with her life. One evening, her husband came back from work with some unexpected news. Yasmin recalls, 'He said, "You know you're bored?" And I said, "Yeah – well not *bored* bored, but I want to do something different." We were considering going off to learn a language this September at college together. Doing something together rather than just doing things on our own. And he said, "Well, I've applied for this thing at the BBC," and that was it! Really, I obviously thought he was joking. I really didn't believe for one minute that he'd applied for this!'

Both Bill and Yasmin worked as nursing staff at the hospital in Cheltenham and Bill had seen a notice pinned up on the staff board asking for volunteers with a medical back-ground to join the project. He came home and announced that he had applied to the BBC to be accepted on the Iron

Jonathan 'Bill' Billinghurst (37)

Born 1963 in Stroud but raised in Cheltenham. Married Yasmin in December 1993. Father of Laszlo and Rosie. After leaving school had various jobs, including as an oven cleaner, caretaker and pork butcher. Joined the NHS in 1984, first as an orderly then as an operating theatre assistant. Interests include football coaching and photography.

Yasmin Billinghurst (36)

Born 1964 in Birmingham. Married to Bill and mother of Laszlo, Rosie and an older daughter Naomi, currently at college. Trained as a nurse in 1993 including working in an eye theatre. Returned to nursing in June 1997, working in an oph-thalmic and maxillo-facial surgery ward. Her job involves all aspects of patient care – including making endless cups of tea!

Laszlo Billinghurst (5)

Born 1995 in Cheltenham. Son of Bill and Yasmin. Started Holy Trinity elementary school in September 1999. His hobbies include drawing, colouring and building anything in Lego. Owns a dog called Bell, which he missed. Most of all, he wanted to make himself a bow and arrow in the Iron Age – which he did.

Rosie Billinghurst (4)

Born 1996 in Cheltenham. Daughter of Bill and Yasmin. Joined her brother at elementary school in September 2000, but only for 10 days before going back to the Iron Age. Loves cooking and doing anything around the house to help her mum. Missed her cat Kipling. Most wanted to make mud pies in the Iron Age – which she did.

Age project. Yasmin's first reaction was utter amazement. 'At first, to be perfectly honest with you, I thought it was the most stupid thing I'd ever heard of. I couldn't possibly imagine living in a mud hut, because this is what I perceived. Mud hut, children covered and caked in filth. Freezing cold November time. He must be stark raving mad. But as the weeks have gone by, I just feel it's great, absolutely great. I've really got into the idea big time.'

Ron and Brenda Phillips are also parents, but their son and daughter have long left home. They were the oldest people on the project, aged 59 and 58 respectively, and are blacksmiths living in the Stoke-on-Trent area. Ron was excited at the prospect of trying to smelt and forge iron using Iron Age techniques. 'It just seems fascinating to me. You work with iron, you are a blacksmith, and here you're going to be living and breathing the Iron Age. One of the fascinations of working iron is the fact that we're using the same tools as they used literally thousands of years ago. The tools didn't really evolve. The ones that we are using today are absolutely identical in every form to what they used thousands of years ago.'

Ron Phillips (59)

Born 1941 in Stafford. Married to Brenda, with two children and two grandchildren. Became fascinated with blacksmithing in his youth. Trained for six years in engineering before becoming a blacksmith. Built steam traction engines as a hobby in his spare time. Interests include camping, narrowboating, caravanning, reading, history and walking.

Brenda Phillips (58)

Born 1942 in Chesterfield. Married Ron in 1963. They celebrated their 37th wedding anniversary during the project. Left school at 15 and went into computing, working in data preparation offices. She has a son Darren and a daughter Mandy, and grandchildren Stuart and Amy. Interests include gardening, computing, walking, camping and working in Ron's forge.

Rather like Anne Rickard, Brenda was more concerned about some of the practical problems of living in Iron Age conditions, although both she and Ron had spent many holidays camping as a family. 'I like old things, I like thinking about what happened in the past. I get nostalgic about my childhood, you know, going back thinking how we used to live. You can dress up in all sorts, but going back to the Iron Age – I was never really sure what they wore. I've got an idea now and it's exciting, to think you can wear exactly what they used to wear and to know how they felt, in long dresses when it's muddy and pouring with rain.'

Brenda also had concerns about the long, dark nights living in roundhouses built on the site of an original Iron Age hillfort. 'I'm thinking the houses will be dark inside apart from candles and you're going to have shadows. And I'm thinking I hope the spirits don't come back, because we're on the actual site. It's going to be a bit eerie but it's also going to be exciting because you just never know what could happen, being on an actual site. I mean it probably sounds silly and stupid, but you just don't know … '

The remaining four volunteers joined the project as single people. Nik Stanbury lived for many years in Pembrokeshire and he was already familiar with the site. However, he had recently moved to North Yorkshire, where he started a business designing and making fine quality metalwork and jewellery. He also enjoys walking and camping. Perhaps because he was joining the project as a single person, Nik had given a lot of thought to the challenge of living in a new community. 'I'm looking forward to being outside, first and foremost, and living as naturally as possible. I'm also looking forward to being part of an enforced community, which is probably quite a strange thing to say. I think that's going to be fascinating. I'm also looking forward to picking up other people's skills, like blacksmithing. Now, what I know about blacksmithing, you could probably write on the back of a postage stamp – and it would actually decrease the value of the postage stamp!'

The other single male was Chris Park, another artist who had completed a BA degree in Fine Art and Sculpture. However, he became disillusioned with the art world and chose to pursue other interests, which included being an environmental volunteer protecting sea turtles in Greece. He spent his time camping on the coastal dunes before following a variety of other jobs which were very relevant to life in the Iron Age. These included working in complementary medicine, tree planting, goat herding in France and living in a co-operative on an organic farm in Carmarthenshire. However, his real interest in the project stemmed from his personal spirituality, which is influenced by traditional and contemporary paganism, druidry and modern witchcraft. He first heard about the project whilst attending a druid camp. 'I'm used to living in a community and the idea just

Nik Stanbury (43)

Born in 1957 in Kingston upon Thames, Surrey but raised in west Wales when not at boarding school. Trained for a BA Hons. in Silversmithing and Three-Dimensional Design, and at the Victoria and Albert Museum for a PhD in Japanese Shakudo and Shibuichi Alloys. His interests include walking, camping, music and playing the saxophone.

Chris Park (27)

Born 1973 in Henley-on-Thames but raised in Stokenchurch in the Chilterns. Trained as a sculptor and artist before studying Contemporary Religion at Bath Spa University College. Widely travelled with a wide range of jobs in Britain and overseas. Trained with the International Rescue Corps. Practises yoga and herbal medicine and is an active member of several druid orders.

seemed to spark something inside me. My spirituality is very much grounded in the natural environment. I still see beauty in cities and people and technology, yet fundamentally I think I need to have those spiritual connections with the natural environment. It's really important for my own sense of place and sense of who I am.'

Because of his interest in paganism and druidism, Chris looked forward to the experience in spiritual terms. 'For an Iron Age community, I think the centre would have been some spiritual focus, maybe, or something well connected to their natural environment … It would have been a powerful thing for them. Today we seem to try and control our world and you know, we're quite divorced from it. But I think it will be a really nice experience, to meet the world in that kind of way, as a group. Living on the land, with animals and the elements. I think it'll be very interesting to see how it works.'

Bethan Jones was a young single woman who joined the project as teacher to the children. In contrast to Chris Park, she is a devout Christian. Her first language is Welsh and she only started to learn English at the age of four. Bethan was a history teacher and also worked as an Education Assistant at the Museum of Welsh Life at St Fagan's near Cardiff where there are Iron Age roundhouses on display. She became well-known there as the only person who needed firelighters to light a fire. She also boycotted the restaurant when she realized that the pigs she had nurtured since they were born had been sent off for slaughtering. Of all the people selected, Bethan was well aware of the realities of living in the Iron Age. 'I think it'll be horrendous. I think it's going to be really horrific. I think we're all going to be so shocked when we go into these Iron Age houses. I mean, I like my bed. I like my luxuries in life and to be without them for seven weeks – I think I'm going to struggle. But it's also going to be quite enlightening … What can I do without, you know? It's going to make us realize we can do without these things … like, shampoo isn't a necessity, it's a luxury. But I'm looking forward to it really.'

Bethan Jones (25)

Born in 1975 in Llanelli, south Wales. First language is Welsh. Studied Welsh History at Cardiff University before taking a teaching diploma. Taught history at a secondary school then decided to take time off to travel. A committed Christian, her main interests are playing the piano, drama, reading, cinema, netball and 'always looking for the next adventure'.

Emma Wooster was the seventeenth member of the group. She studied radio and television production at the University of the West of England in Bristol, combined with a course on Social Anthropology. In her own words, 'three years later I left university with a degree and a husband, Richard.' Emma has since worked on many popular BBC series, including *Vets in Practice, Holiday Reps, Marry Me* and *Holiday Swaps*. In many ways, Emma had the most difficult job of all: she was not only expected to live in the Iron Age conditions, but she also had to film for the series when the main television crew was not on location. The opportunity the project offered had to be balanced with some very real private concerns. 'It's a risk … this could completely ruin my career or it could completely change the direction that I go in. And that's what excites me about it, really. When I was at university I did a degree in social anthropology and film-making and up until now I haven't been able to put that into practice. This is the closest that I've come to a project like this. When I got the call and they asked me if I would consider it, it was initially a 'no'. But I spoke to my friends and my family and they said 'yes'. They think it would be a really good thing for me to do.'

Emma Wooster (29)

Born 1970 in Pill near Bristol. Studied for a degree in Time Based Media at the UWE. She joined the BBC, first working on Radio 1 before becoming a television researcher, then a director, working on series such as *Vets in Practice, Holiday Reps* and *Marry Me*. She lives in Bristol with her husband and three cats – LB, LG and Jet. She has recently taken up rollerblading.

Together, these fourteen adults and three children had a wide diversity of experience. There were two blacksmiths and a silversmith, several experienced campers and an ex-butcher; six people had had experience of rearing their own livestock and were at least partially self-sufficient. Several of the volunteers had travelled to remote parts of the world, one was a consultant ecologist and lectured on sustainable development, another had worked as a chef, two were trained nurses, one was a history teacher with a knowledge of the Iron Age, and several were talented musicians.

As a group, these people had the skills needed to survive in the Iron Age, provided they worked effectively as a team, organized themselves and shared their collective knowledge and experience. But only the next seven weeks would tell.

◁◁ A stone artefact embellished with spiral carvings, found at the Neolithic site of Skara Brae on the Orkney Islands.
◁ A highly romanticized coloured aquatint from the early nineteenth century of an archdruid in his judicial habit.
▽ A Druid stone circle situated just north of Inverness, in the Highland region of Scotland.

3

Life Before Iron

TWELVE THOUSAND YEARS AGO THE LAST MAJOR ICE AGE in Europe was coming to an end. Previously, most of northern Europe had been covered in hundreds of metres of ice, but the period between 10,000 and 4000 BC was a time when the climate became progressively warmer. As the great European ice cap began to retreat, so tundra replaced ice and bare rock over the British Isles and herds of reindeer began grazing on the sparse vegetation. As the climate warmed still further, so red and roe deer, wild pigs and elk spread from southern Europe. Initially birch, pine and hazel woodland became established, to be replaced by oak, elm and lime as conditions continued to become warmer still.

In London alone, fossils of the straight-tusked elephant (now extinct), lion, hippopotamus and the spotted hyena have been found where they lived during warm periods. At cooler times, the giant deer, the mammoth and the woolly rhinoceros (all now extinct) moved in to colonize the region.

Although early man had previously lived in the region, the last Ice Age had forced him further south. Now the improving climatic conditions encouraged early Mesolithic hunter-gatherers of the Middle Stone Age to migrate northwards across the continent of Europe. Because much of the world's moisture was still locked up as ice, the global sea level was lower than that of the present day. The region we know as the British Isles was joined to the continent of Europe, and the North Sea was a region of low-lying fenland with the river Thames a tributary of the Rhine. This landbridge allowed early hunter-gatherers to migrate from present-day Denmark to colonize the British region. By 7500 BC, the Mesolithic population of Britain was probably around 10,000 individuals, comprising isolated family groups of between 20 and 50 people living roughly 300 kilometres (185 miles) apart. These early people made sophisticated tools from bone, antler and wood, which included flint and chert saws, knives, axes, fine stone arrowheads, spears and harpoons. They also navigated rivers and lakes in canoes made from hollowed tree trunks.

land about 7000 BC

modern coastline

North Sea

Sometime after 6000 BC, the landbridge connecting the region to the rest of Europe was flooded by rising sea level and Britain became an island. Inevitably, the people became more insular and developed a tendency to absorb and adapt the cultures which were developing elsewhere on the continent, rather than participating fully in their evolution. This characteristic still rings true today.

By 4000 BC, the farming techniques of the Neolithic people of the later Stone Age began to spread into Britain by a process which archaeologists call acculturation. At first they used slash and burn techniques to clear land, before moving on to cultivate fresh ground. They gradually changed from this shifting cultivation to live in stable communities and built rectangular or round wooden dwellings which housed an extended family or perhaps a small community.

They also learnt to make finger-moulded pottery and to mine flint with antler picks. They probably wore simple garments made from animal skins, as they might not have known how to weave cloth. Most importantly, they used refined stone implements which allowed them to clear land and cultivate cereal crops such as wheat and barley. They also began to domesticate sheep, pigs and cattle. They concentrated on farming the lighter, upland soils where the woodland was thinnest and avoided the thickly wooded valley bottoms where the soil was heavy and difficult to work. This means that some of the areas of heaviest settlement are found on the chalk downlands of southern Britain. Over a period of many generations these people gradually began to change the landscape of Britain.

Even though Neolithic communities were relatively small, they were sufficiently well organized to build large constructions which required group participation. Some of the oldest remains in the British landscape are at sites known as causewayed camps, dating from around 3500 BC. These were probably used for a number of purposes, including as a community gathering site, a livestock pen and a trading centre, as well as a religious site and ceremonial arena. The best preserved, and probably the most important camp archaeologically, is at Windmill Hill near Avebury in Wiltshire.

Neolithic people also built communal tombs called long barrows, which are roughly contemporary with the causewayed camps. The barrows were large structures up to 100 metres (330 feet) long and oriented roughly east-west, which suggests that the rising sun was important in Neolithic religions. They were either made of earth (earthen long barrows) or built with a chamber of large stones (megalithic or chambered long barrows). Neolithic religious activity probably centred on a cult of the ancestors and the bones of the dead were often used in their religious ceremonies. The dead were sometimes interred after all the flesh had rotted off their bones, in a ritual called excarnation. Occasionally the bones were also burnt in some form of cremation ceremony.

As early as 3300 BC standing stones arranged in a circle or a flattened oval began to be erected around the British Isles, although most of them were built during the late Neolithic and early Bronze Age. At least 900 of these stone circles still exist, the most famous being Stonehenge. Other impressive stone circles in Britain include Avebury in Wiltshire, the Rollright Stones in Oxfordshire and Castlerigg in Cumbria. These sites probably evolved from causewayed camps and earlier henges. Neolithic henges are simple structures of banks and ditches enclosing

▽ Stone circles probably evolved from earlier wooden henges and causewayed camps. By 2000 BC, Stonehenge had become the site it is today, the most famous Bronze Age monument in Europe.

an area of land up to 12 hectares (30 acres), but unlike defensive structures which had the ditch *outside* the bank, the henges were built with the ditch *inside* the bank. This suggests they were probably religious and ceremonial sites rather than defensive enclosures. Some henges show signs of having had stone or wooden circles within them and the first building phase of Stonehenge belongs to this class of monument.

The most common prehistoric monuments in Britain are barrow mounds, and over 6000 have been discovered in the Wessex region (central southern England) alone. Dating from around 2200 BC, barrow mounds are very different from the earlier long barrows in that they are mainly burial places for *individuals* rather than groups and often contain elaborate grave goods giving an indication of the high status of the interred body. These grave goods are the first evidence of a belief in the afterlife. This period also marked the beginning of a new and revolutionary stage in the evolution of societies – the ability to make tools and weapons from metal.

The technique of smelting copper from ore was a remarkable development which defined a new level in man's control over his environment and resources. Later it was found that adding approximately one part tin to nine parts copper produced bronze, which was a much harder metal than pure copper and much more useful for the manufacture of tools and weapons. The alloying of copper with tin heralded the beginning of the European Bronze Age around 2500–2300 BC.

The science of smelting metallic ore and converting it into a variety of metallic artefacts required a much greater degree of labour specialization than was required to work flint and stone. Mining techniques had to be developed to extract the ore and the organization required to bring ore and fuel together on an industrial scale was more sophisticated than anything known previously. This required a well organized trading system of both metal ingots and finished artefacts. It was during the Bronze Age that specialist metal smiths appeared and this increase in the division of labour led to the establishment of the first political organizations.

In Britain, the Bronze Age lasted from around 2500 to 650 BC and the period saw many important social changes. A patriarchal, warlike society began to develop and the concept of an individual warrior-chieftain became established, in contrast to the more community-orientated Neolithic society. Perhaps because of the increase in perceived violence, people also began to live grouped together in enclosed settlements.

This was the first agrarian society which was able to support a growing population; consequently more land was used to grow cereals and livestock and this progressively opened up the British countryside. These early Britons lived in roundhouses and, by the end of the Bronze Age and the beginning of the Iron Age, settlements with perimeter walls, gates and protective palisades began to appear. Craftsmen began to master more sophisticated metalworking using bronze, and these skills were later developed to master the much more challenging science of smelting iron from ore. The age of iron had arrived.

▽ The burning wicker man packed with humans and animals is one of the most enduring and gruesome anecdotes from the Iron Age, but nobody can be absolutely sure that the early Celts really indulged in such practices.

4

The Age of Iron

THE HISTORY OF THE CELTIC PEOPLE is full of contrast: the highlights are brilliant and the shade is menacing. They certainly developed a reputation as warlike, ferocious, squabbling barbarians and they were both feared and respected by the Greeks and Romans. Julius Caesar wrote admiringly of the prowess of the Celtic charioteer, who combined 'the mobility of the cavalry with the staying-power of the infantry', and also of the giant wicker men whose limbs were filled with living people to be ritually sacrificed in flames. Others wrote about their human sacrifice, the alleged promiscuity of their women and the magical rites performed by their religious leaders, the druids.

Yet there was also a highly resourceful and cultured side to the Celtic character. The Celts created an artistic brilliance never before seen in prehistoric Europe. They developed a distinctive, highly stylized, curvilinear form of art and produced elegant figurines and jewellery in bronze and rare metals. They also established a complex and sophisticated proto-feudal society based on sustainable agriculture. But perhaps more than anything else, they are remembered for their mastery in working iron. Yet until the middle of the first millennium BC, nothing was known by the people of the civilized Mediterranean world about the 'barbarians' who inhabited the region north of the Alps.

△ This late Iron Age bronze mirror was discovered in 1908 near Desborough in Northamptonshire and dates from the first century AD. It is a fine example of the famous Celtic curvilinear art. The complex designs were probably traced out with a pair of compasses.

CHRONOLOGY

The Iron Age people did not have a written language and this complicates any attempt to establish a chronology for the period. Before the Romans first arrived in Britain in 55 BC, very little was known of the history of the region and, remarkably, not one single Briton was known by name before that time. This is an extraordinary situation when compared to our knowledge of the Greeks, Romans, Egyptians, Assyrians and other early civilizations, all of which pre-date Iron Age Britain, some by a thousand years or more.

Radiocarbon analysis has revolutionized the dating of artefacts and is vital for establishing dates in the earlier stages of prehistory. However, margins of error in dating the Iron Age period are sometimes too great for this form of analysis to be of much value.

Tree ring analysis, or dendrochronology, has been used since 1901 and is very useful in trying to establish dates during the Iron Age period. The technique works on the principle that the seasonal growth rings of trees create a permanent record in timber which is as unique as a fingerprint. Wooden objects can be accurately dated as far back as 7000 years. Unfortunately, wooden artefacts from the Iron Age, such as shields or chariots, are rarely found in a well-preserved condition. Therefore, although tree ring analysis can be a very effective dating technique, it too has only limited use in the Iron Age.

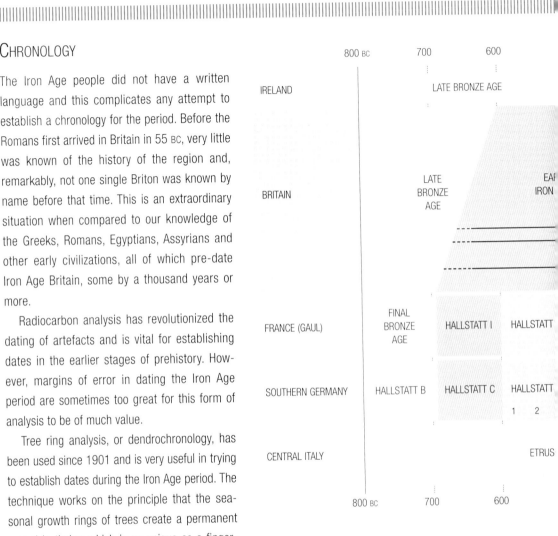

To establish dates in the Iron Age, archaeologists have therefore to rely mainly on identifying a stratigraphic sequence which gives a *relative* chronology of successive periods of human occupation. The earliest attempts to establish a chronology were made in the nineteenth century, when the prehistory of Europe was defined by the

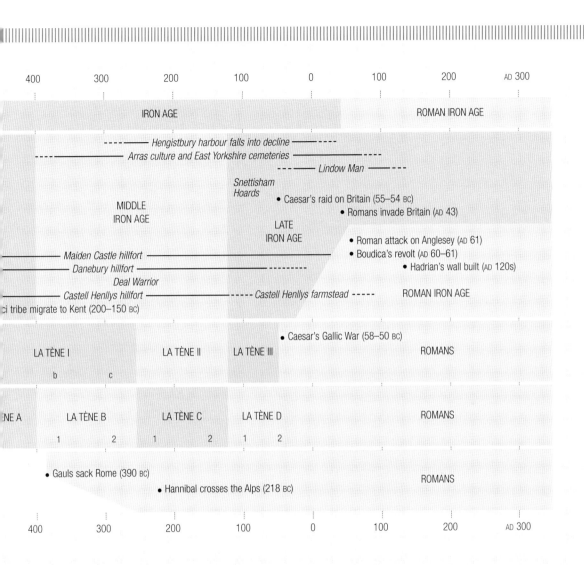

| 400 | 300 | 200 | 100 | 0 | 100 | 200 | AD 300 |

IRON AGE — **ROMAN IRON AGE**

------- Hengistbury harbour falls into decline -------
------- Arras culture and East Yorkshire cemeteries -------
------- Lindow Man -------

Snettisham
Hoards
• Caesar's raid on Britain (55–54 BC)
• Romans invade Britain (AD 43)

MIDDLE
IRON AGE

LATE
IRON AGE
• Roman attack on Anglesey (AD 61)
• Boudica's revolt (AD 60–61)

——— Maiden Castle hillfort ———
——— Danebury hillfort ——— • Hadrian's wall built (AD 120s)
Deal Warrior
——— Castell Henllys hillfort ——— ----- Castell Henllys farmstead ----- ROMAN IRON AGE
ci tribe migrate to Kent (200–150 BC)

• Caesar's Gallic War (58–50 BC)

| LA TÈNE I | LA TÈNE II | LA TÈNE III | ROMANS |
| b | c | | |

| NE A | LA TÈNE B | LA TÈNE C | LA TÈNE D | ROMANS |
| | 1 | 2 | 1 | 2 | 1 | 2 | |

• Gauls sack Rome (390 BC)
ROMANS
• Hannibal crosses the Alps (218 BC)

| 400 | 300 | 200 | 100 | 0 | 100 | 200 | AD 300 |

materials used to make basic tools: hence the Stone, Bronze and Iron Ages.

In 1872, the Iron Age was further divided into distinct periods following important discoveries which identified stylistic differences in ornaments and weapons found at two important sites in central Europe. The first period took its name from a large cemetery found at Hallstatt in Austria (see illustration, page 169), and the second from a site called La Tène on the shores of Lake Neuchâtel in Switzerland. These two places became 'type-sites', where the artefacts were found to be broadly typical of their respective periods (see the diagram above).

▽ The likely distribution of tribes in Celtic Britain around the time of Julius Caesar's abortive raid in 55 BC. The groupings were probably temporary and most of the tribal names listed by Caesar had disappeared when the Romans returned in AD 43.

0		50 miles
0		100 km

TAEZALI

CALEDONES

VENICONES

DAMNONII

North Sea

SELGOVAE

Hadrian's Wall

BRIGANTES

Irish Sea

PARISI

Anglesey

DECEANGLI

CORITANI

ICENI

ORDOVICES

TRINOVANTES

Colchester

•Castell Henllys

CATUVELLAUNI

St Albans

SILURES

London

Canterbury

DUMNONII

Danebury

CANTIACI

DUROTRIGES

ATREBATES

Maiden Castle

Hengistbury Head

English Channel

The Celts were apparently dispersed across the continent by 500 BC and had probably occupied Central Europe for several hundreds, if not thousands, of years before that. They embraced the early techniques of iron working developed in the Middle East and refined them to the point where iron replaced bronze as the metal of choice for tools and weaponry.

Although the Celts probably had a common ancestry, shared a common language root and had a similar cultural background, they probably did not consider themselves to be a single nation or even a 'Celtic commonwealth'. Instead, they would have been far more concerned about their identity at a local or tribal level. It was the Greeks and Romans who saw these people as a single entity – and feared them. The Greeks called them *Keltoi*, meaning 'barbarian', which gave them their modern name. The Romans called them *Celtae*, *Galli* and *Galatae* and chose to classify them into convenient tribal groups. For example, in Britain there were many Celtic tribes, sub-tribes and clans, and the Romans gave them a variety of names such as the 'Silures' or the 'Iceni', which might have had only a vague resemblance to their original names and tribal groupings. In fact, the tribal factions were probably temporary and unstable, fragmenting or fusing according to outside influences.

At their peak, the European Celts were an expansionist force. Around 400 BC, a group migrated south across the Alps and settled in the Po valley in northern Italy. In 390 BC, the Gallic 'Senones' tribe attacked and sacked Rome. Although they were eventually driven back to the Po valley, they had developed a reputation as a fearsome, barbaric neighbour. The Celts also invaded the Balkans and in 279 BC attacked Delphi, the most important shrine in Greece. Although they too were eventually beaten back by the Greeks, some moved on to Turkey where they became known as the *Galatae*.

Our understanding of Celtic history comes from archaeological and linguistic evidence, from the writings of the Greeks and Romans and from stories passed down through the ages in an oral tradition. (The Celtic druid priests could read and write in Latin and Greek, but their religious vows forbade them from committing any of their knowledge to paper.) These sources all have their limitations.

The leading Classical writers, including Julius Caesar, Strabo, Posidonius and Diodorus Siculus, wrote extensively about the Iron Age people. Although their records give us a valuable insight into Celtic life, their view of the 'barbarians' was inevitably distorted by their own experience. The Romans tended to concentrate on political and military power and often wanted to impress their masters back in Rome, so a little exaggeration in their writings was not unusual. They also had a tendency to stress those elements of Celtic life which were exotic, weird or titillating – and especially anything to do with the role of women or religion. They were horrified, for example, by the practice of human sacrifice, despite their condonation (and even enjoyment) of what went on back home in the Colosseum.

Many Celtic legends and myths have been passed down through countless generations in Ireland and have been preserved in ancient Irish texts. The Romans never actually invaded Ireland, so the Celtic Iron Age traditions lasted there much longer than in Britain. These stories were eventually written down by the Christian monks, but not until the seventh and eighth centuries AD, so their accuracy must also be questioned. Unfortunately many of the Irish texts have been lost, so this documentary evidence is incomplete.

The archaeologist R.J.C. Atkinson wrote that 'the raw material of prehistory is not men, but things,' and archaeological evidence certainly provides a vast amount of information about the Iron Age. However, the challenge and excitement of the subject are also its greatest limitation, for the evidence found by excavation is inevitably sporadic and the survival of artefacts is a lottery. There are literally hundreds of hillforts in Britain and thousands of smaller farmsteads, yet only a handful of these sites have been subjected to detailed excavation. The archaeological evidence of the Celtic lifestyle is often found in the form of grave goods buried with the dead or at special sites where religious offerings were made – usually in rivers, lakes or waterlogged sites such as bogs. Metalwork usually survives as rusted iron or corroded bronze. Organic materials such as wood, cloth and bone rarely survive after two thousand years in the ground, except in exceptional conditions such as in waterlogged soil. Very occasionally, whole human bodies are found in boggy conditions where the tannic acid and anaerobic conditions act to preserve organic material. These remains tell us something about the clothing the Celtic people wore, the food they ate, and even the type of body tattoo that was fashionable during the Iron Age period. But how representative these few remains are of the millions of people who were born, lived and died during the period is difficult to establish.

Finally, there is linguistic evidence, including Celtic words in the Classical texts and surviving Celtic place names. Linguists have identified six distinct Celtic languages divided into two families. The 'P-Celtic' or Brithonic languages include

Welsh, Cornish and Breton and are thought to originate from the original ancient British tongue. The 'Q-Celtic' or Goidelic include Irish, Scottish Gaelic and Manx, which find their roots in old Irish. Linguistic research has shown that the indigenous language of the early Britons and Irish is closely related to that of the early Gauls.

The Greeks and Romans wrote many detailed eyewitness accounts of the Celts. Unfortunately, they had little understanding of Celtic culture and had a vested interest in elaborating upon the fierce and brutish nature of these people. Trying to understand the Celts from the writings of these Classical authors is rather like trying to understand Persian culture from old copies of British tabloid press stories written about Saddam Hussein during the Gulf War. The Greek writer Diodorus Siculus colourfully described how the Celts cut off their enemies' heads and nailed them over the doors of their huts. 'In exactly the same way as hunters do with their skulls of the animals they have slain … they preserved the heads of their most high-ranking victims in cedar oil, keeping them carefully in wooden boxes.'

Despite some of these more sensational anecdotes, the Greek and Roman writers – and especially Julius Caesar – give us a valuable insight into the Celtic way of life. Diodorus also gave a graphic but derisory description of the British Iron Age Celt. 'Their aspect is terrifying … They are very tall in stature, with rippling muscles under clear white skin. Their hair is blond, but not naturally so: they bleach it, to this day, artificially, washing it in lime and combing it back from their foreheads. They look like wood-demons, their hair thick and shaggy like a horse's mane. Some of them are clean shaven, but others – especially those of high rank – shave their cheeks but leave a moustache that covers the whole mouth and, when they eat and drink, acts like a sieve, trapping particles of food …'

△ Julius Caesar (100–44 BC) wrote the first eye-witness accounts of life in Celtic Britain. However, because of the political situation back in Rome, he might have been guilty of exaggeration, embellishment or distortion.

49

WHAT THE CLASSICAL WRITERS SAID ABOUT THE CELTS

Most of the descriptions of the lifestyle, dress, social behaviour and military strategy of the Iron Age people come from the Roman and Greek writers. The most famous is undoubtedly Julius Caesar (100–44 BC) who made a daring but ultimately disastrous attempt to invade the British Islands in 55 and 54 BC. His conquest of Gaul between 58 and 51 BC gave him prestige and wealth and his *Commentaries* (more commonly known as the *Gallic War*) tend to justify his actions, many of which were actually illegal. His writings therefore have an inevitable bias but they do give a detailed and valuable account of Celtic Europe immediately prior to the Christian era.

Although the classical writers wrote mostly about the continental Celts, many of their observations would have been equally appropriate in Britain.

The Greek historian Strabo (c.64 BC to AD 21) wrote about the Iron Age farmer in Britain: 'Their cities are the forests, for they fell trees and fence in large enclosures in which they build huts and pen in their cattle, but not for any great length of time. The weather tends to rain rather than snow. Mist is very common, so that for whole days at a stretch the sun is seen only for three or four hours around midday'. Strabo also wrote about conditions in Gaul: 'And none of the country is untilled except parts where tilling is precluded by swamps and woods. Yet these parts too are thickly peopled – more because of the largeness of the population than because of the industry of the people.'

The Greek politician Polybius (c.200 to c.118 BC) wrote extensively about the Celts in northern Italy. 'They lived in unwalled villages, without any superfluous furniture … they slept on beds of leaves and fed on meat and were exclusively occupied with war and agriculture.' And the civil servant Herodian (AD 180–238) wrote, 'Most of Britain is marshland, since it is flooded by the ocean tides. It is the custom of the barbarians to swim in these swamps, or to run in them submerged to the waist. Because the greater part of the body is naked they do not mind the mud.'

The success and wealth of the prehistoric Celtic culture were based on the Celts' ability to maintain a strong social structure, which in part was due to their mastery of iron-making technology. Iron is a common element found in the earth's crust, but it almost always occurs as a compound. Very occasionally, metallic iron is found in its natural state, for example in an iron meteorite from space. These rare iron meteorites provided a 'magical' source of the metal before the technique of smelting ore was understood. Such rare occurrences allowed a few smiths to discover the valuable properties of iron thousands of years prior to the Iron Age. For example, iron beads made from meteoric iron and shaped by rubbing with stone implements were worn in Egypt as early as 4000 BC.

The problem with trying to identify the very beginning of iron manufacture in the archaeological record is that finds of early iron implements are not well documented. This is partly because early excavators tended to pay little interest to iron finds (gold, silver and bronze artefacts were much more exciting), and partly because iron has a habit of rusting away. The best authenticated early iron discovery comes from a burial dated around the middle of the third millennium BC in an early Bronze Age town near Ankara in central Turkey. Among a collection of grave goods, which included a bronze stag inlaid with silver and pottery and metal vessels, was a dagger with a short iron blade. The hilt was organic (probably wood) and had been overlaid with gold sheet. This burial site has been dated between 2500 and 2300 BC, which coincides with the beginning of the Bronze Age in Britain.

These early discoveries suggest that iron-making technology was in its infancy over much of modern Asia Minor by the end of the third millennium BC. Although iron was probably only produced in small quantities (hence its association with other high-value burial goods), the knowledge and understanding of how to work the metal was sufficiently well advanced to produce serviceable tools and weapons by about 2500 BC. During the second millennium BC there is written evidence of the use of iron, found on clay tablets dating back to the seventeenth century BC excavated in the Hittite capital of Bogazköy and the ancient city of Kültepe. The writing on the tablets gives details of trading and it is possible to calculate the relative value by weight of the different metals being traded. (The merchants using these tablets were dealing on behalf of kings and aristocracy in highly prestigious goods such as copper, tin and lapis lazuli.) One commodity stands out as being of particular value and was worth *five* times the price of gold – it was iron.

Other written evidence suggests that even quite small iron items such as dagger blades had such a high status that they made worthy royal gifts, and it is possible that iron production was kept under royal control because of its high prestige value. Old Assyrian letters have come to light which discuss the trade of tin between Assur and Kültepe and the writings also refer to a metal called *amutum*, which is generally identified as iron; its value was 40 times that of silver and it was 400 times more expensive than tin.

Iron is a relatively soft metal, and the manufacture of steel was an important development because it allowed a much harder cutting edge to be produced. Iron needs to be alloyed with a small amount of carbon to produce steel and this is achieved in a crude manner by heating the blade of the iron implement in a charcoal furnace, hammering it when hot, and then quenching it with water. Carbon is absorbed into the surface of the iron during this process, but it has to be repeated several times before sufficient carbon is absorbed to produce a veneer of steel.

The use of smelted iron ornaments and ceremonial weapons became more common during the period from 1900 to 1400 BC. At about this time the Hittites invented the technique of tempering iron, which hardens and toughens the metal by heating, sudden cooling and re-heating. Iron is far more robust than bronze or other copper alloys. Consequently, armies with iron weapons had an advantage over their opponents. Iron agricultural implements allowed more land to be cultivated and to be more intensively farmed. Not surprisingly, the Hittite kings might have kept their ironworking techniques secret and restricted the export of iron weapons.

Tutankhamen's tomb was found to contain two daggers, one of gold and the other of iron shaped by hammering. The iron weapon was made prior to 1350 BC, but is thought not to have originated from Egypt but from the Hittite empire. The Hittites never used the metal extensively, but they produced limited quantities of iron daggers and swords before their empire collapsed around 1200 BC.

By this time, most of the successful Bronze Age civilizations in the eastern Mediterranean were beginning to decline. This was a period of widespread unrest and waves of migrants spread through the Middle East and southern Europe. At first, iron implements were scarce, but the period around 1000 BC marks the beginning of the Iron Age proper in this region, when iron began to replace bronze as the basic material for implements and weapons. It is the last stage of the archaeological three-age system (Stone, Bronze and Iron Ages), but chronologically the term is only of local value because iron took the place of bronze at different times in different cultures.

In Cyprus, the change from bronze to iron occurred very quickly in a matter of only 150 years or so. By 1050 BC, Cyprus, Crete and mainland Greece as far north as Macedonia were fully in the Iron Age. Some archaeologists have argued that this rapid transition did not come about simply because of the superior quality of iron for making tools and weapons, as its relative advantages had been known for centuries. Instead, the change might have occurred because of a drastic shortage of bronze (or of tin to make bronze), forcing people to use iron regardless of their preference.

In the rest of south-eastern Europe, an iron industry had developed between 1100 and 800 BC, but bronze weapons remained dominant and the transition to iron took longer than in Greece and Cyprus. This might have been because supplies of copper and tin were plentiful, or perhaps the iron-smiths could not yet produce weapons as good as those of bronze. The production of iron also required more labour and more fuel than bronze, and this might also have been a limiting factor.

As iron production became more widespread throughout Europe and the Middle East, so the value of the metal fell. In the nineteenth century BC, iron was worth 40 times more than silver by weight. By the seventh century BC in Greece, silver bought 2000 times its weight in iron; in other words, iron had become 80,000 times cheaper in relation to silver over a period of just over 1000 years.

As the Romans developed large-scale iron production, so the value of iron continued to fall. When Julius Caesar led a raid into southern Britain in 54 BC, he discovered a small-scale iron industry in the Weald, an area of chalk downs lying to the south of London. This industry was developed further after the Roman invasion in AD 43 and very soon they increased production at least ten-fold. Within a relatively short time, the region had become the major source of iron for Roman military hardware, and their armies and navies in north-western Europe obtained all their nails, tools and miscellaneous building iron from at least 67 iron-making sites in southern England.

Whatever tales the Romans may have spun to impress their compatriots back home, it seems they knew Britain was not the barbaric place they made it out to be – on the contrary, it was a country of organized industry and skilled craftsmen.

◁◁ The latrine was specially built for the project. The modesty walls were built over a sunken concrete cesspit – far superior to anything the Iron Age Celts would have used!

◁ Water was obtained from a mains tap initially located down by the river. After a week it was relocated at the top of the hill.

▽ The largest of the four roundhouses at Castell Henllys was completed only a few months before filming began. An angle of 45 degrees has been found to be the optimum pitch for the roof. Anything less does not shed rainwater effectively and anything greater increases the area of thatch with no added benefit.

5

The Week the Country Ran Dry

THE IRONY OF A FUEL CRISIS THAT NEARLY brought Britain to a standstill coinciding with the beginning of the Iron Age project was not lost on either the volunteers or the BBC production team. It was not an easy start for anyone. David, Anne and Christopher Rickard managed to find enough petrol to get them from Dorset to Pembrokeshire by car, but most of the other volunteers had to make other arrangements at the last minute and travel by train. So rather than meeting up as planned at a local hotel, most of the volunteers met their fellow associates on a local train, somewhere between Swansea station and the tiny halt of Clynderwen. (It was not difficult to identify each other because they were the only people on the train carrying empty suitcases – soon to be filled with their twenty-first-century possessions.)

It had also been a frantic week for the production team trying to get everything delivered and up to the site while being rationed to £5 worth of fuel each day by the local garage. By the end of the week, the country was practically at a standstill due to the petrol blockade but, with one or two exceptions, the hillfort was ready. The biggest problem were the chickens. The man who was due to deliver them called to say that he had no petrol at all, so the chickens arrived two days after the volunteers. But everything else was in place by Saturday 16 September, as planned.

That afternoon was a whirlwind for the volunteers. After a buffet lunch which gave everyone the chance to introduce themselves, the afternoon was set aside for briefings and final medical checks. Yasmin Billinghurst announced that she had decided to give up smoking, so she was allowed nicotine patches (classified under the 'Iron Age rules' as prescribed medication). Jody Elphick had been a vegetarian for many years but had decided to start eating meat again. During her parents' year in the Iron Age, one of the women in the group had been a vegetarian and this had created tension and conflict over the allocation of eggs and cheese. Jody very wisely wanted to avoid any similar problems, but it must have been a difficult moral decision for her to take. She did eventually revert to being a vegetarian six weeks later, just a few days before she left the hillfort.

As everyone introduced themselves in turn, Anne Rickard announced that she had written a special song for the occasion and offered to sing it unaccompanied, to the tune of Cliff Richard's *Summer Holiday*.

△ Anne Rickard is a semi-professional singer who performs with an all-women group. Her entertaining rendition of *Celtic Holiday* on their last night in the twenty-first century endeared her to the group.

We're all going on a Celtic holiday,
No more chocolate for a month or two.
There's no shirking on our Celtic holiday,
Or they'll be no dinner for me or you,
For a month or two.

We've been chosen for this Celtic holiday,
'Cos we've shown that we're as mad as you.
What, no knickers on our Celtic holiday?
It could be draughty for me and you,
When the wind blows through.

We're going where the rain falls daily,
We're going where there's no flushing loo.
We've read it all in history,
Now let's see if it's true.

There'll be cameras on our Celtic holiday,
Lenses focusing on me and you.
There's no escaping from this Celtic holiday,
It'll be repeated in a year or two,
On BBC2!

Anne's rendition was a difficult act to follow, but the group still had business to work through. Peter Firstbrook, the series producer, briefed the group on the principles and rules of the project. Martin Pailthorpe, the director, explained some of the filming details and outlined his immediate needs for when the filming started in earnest the following morning. Siobhan Connelly, the BBC's safety adviser, ran through a briefing that included everything from cooking hygiene to how to lift heavy weights safely, and from fire precautions to the special needs of the young children. Late in the afternoon, everybody was taken off to the local doctor's surgery in Newport for a final medical check-up and to have injections against hepatitis A and tetanus. At the time, nobody expected they would be seeing the local GP again quite so quickly.

Phil Bennett, the manager of the Castell Henllys hillfort, gave the last briefing of the afternoon. Phil is an archaeologist by training and had spent the previous eight years developing the site, including the construction of a new roundhouse. Phil was delighted at the prospect of seeing his hillfort inhabited in authentic Iron Age style. However, parts of the site were still under excavation by the University of York and it was important that the volunteers understood which areas they could not venture into. But it was the extraordinary history of the site which fascinated the volunteers, for they were about to move into a hillfort which had been home to Iron Age Celts for over 600 years.

Castell Henllys had been continuously occupied during the Iron Age from about 600 BC until the first century AD. Since archaeological work first began in 1981, the interior and the gateways had been fully excavated. The archaeologists had also found evidence of an adjacent Iron Age farmstead which had been occupied by Celtic people during the early Roman period. Castell Henllys is now the

△ The entrance to Castell Henllys Iron Age hillfort today. The banks and wattle fencing were constructed especially for the filming project.
▷ The hillfort compound today. The first dwelling was built in 1979 and is now the longest-standing reconstructed Iron Age roundhouse in the country.

Compare the pictures on this page with the computer-generated images overleaf of how Castell Henllys would have looked around 300 BC.

N

▽ A computer-generated impression of how Castell Henllys would have looked from the air in around 300 BC. There would have been ten or twelve roundhouses surrounded by a strong wooden palisade. The hill would have been kept clear of trees for defensive reasons.

▷ Castell Henllys today, surrounded by mature deciduous trees. The area to the lower right of the entrance is the current excavation of the first-century AD farmstead, which was established outside the confines of the original hillfort.

▷ The entrance of the hillfort as it might have looked in around 300 BC. In front of the palisade and earth rampart was a deep ditch. Behind the impressive wooden gates was a sophisticated double-entry stone gateway.

▽ The compound of the original Iron Age hillfort would have contained up to a dozen roundhouses. The fort was surrounded by an earth rampart and a strong wooden palisade.

WELCOME TO THE IRON AGE

For the next six and a half weeks you will live in Castell Henllys, a genuine Iron Age hillfort that was home to early Britons for over 600 years. You will live in conditions that are as close to those of the Iron Age as can reasonably be achieved for people from the twenty-first century.

We want you to enjoy your experience, but this unique opportunity comes with certain obligations. Tomorrow morning you will be taken to the settlement. There you will find everything necessary for survival in the Iron Age, including sufficient prepared food for several days. But you must also master the essential skills required to survive in pre-Roman Britain, and master them quickly. By the afternoon you must learn how to look after your livestock, including how to milk your cows and goats. Learn well, for your own wellbeing will depend on them.

Before the sun sets in the west you must also select your chieftain. He or she can be of any age. This person will have an essential function: through them you will be informed of the tasks you are required to perform to survive in the Iron Age. You already have many skills between you. Share your talents well, work together and plan for the future. This will be the secret of your success and happiness.

Your time in the Iron Age will end with the celebration of Samhain – the ancient Celtic festival that falls on 31 October. This festival marks the end of the old year and the beginning of the new. It is also the one day of the year when the veil between the living and the dead is at its thinnest – when those who are long gone from this world can return to join the living. Prepare ahead and celebrate.

Between now and Samhain, you must all master the skills of the Iron Age people. Support and advice on how to survive will be passed to you through your chieftain in messages such as this one. Listen carefully; beware of the perils of the age; and protect your grain and livestock from natural predators.

longest-running archaeological excavation of its kind in the country and is also the only Iron Age site in the British Isles where reconstructed roundhouses have been built *exactly* where the original Iron Age buildings stood. There are now four roundhouses and a granary built on the site and they include the longest-standing reconstructed roundhouse in the country, built in 1989.

The original hillfort was built on a small spur inside the meander of a small river and is therefore classified by archaeologists as a 'promontory fort'. The site is about 0.5 hectares (1.25 acres) in area and surrounded on three sides by steep banks. During the Iron Age, these scarps would have presented a formidable barrier to any invading force. In addition to the steep slopes, the fort was surrounded by defences made up of deep ditches and massive earth ramparts topped with timber palisades (stout wooden fences). To the north-west, where the promontory merged with the valley side, a double earth rampart and palisades joined an impressive defensive stone wall and gatehouse, with a tower and internal guard chambers. Additional defensive outworks of banks and ditches guarded the approaches to the fort.

Even today, the fort is an imposing sight when viewed from the bottom of the hill. During the Iron Age, all the trees and bushes on the steep slopes would have been cut down to give a direct line of sight to potentially hostile visitors. The promontory hill would have looked man-made and this would have further enhanced the status of the owners. Castell Henllys was occupied throughout most of the Iron Age by the extended families related to a local nobleman. Together with their retainers, servants and perhaps slaves, the population would number anything between 50 and 150 people. This was a relatively small hillfort, but it would have dominated the local area and the nobleman would have been able to demand a great deal of local labour in tithes in order to maintain the buildings and defences.

The excavations inside the palisade fence have revealed that the settlement was densely packed with roundhouses and four-post granaries with raised floors. There were probably ten roundhouses at any one time, although they would have required regular rebuilding as the wooden posts rotted in the ground. The granaries, combined with the discovery of a wide range of carbonized seeds from various cereal crops grown locally, give the impression that the hillfort was used as a storage site for surplus grain. This suggests that only high-status families lived in the settlement and the grain might have been brought in by lower-status families as a tithe or tax. If this was the case, then the labour needed for building and maintaining the defences and the gateways might also have been provided by local people as a tribute payment.

The Iron Age was undoubtedly a violent time, but the elaborate fortifications at Castell Henllys were probably much too extensive for them to be justified solely for defence. Archaeologists now believe these fortifications have more to do with the need for local rulers to show off their power and prestige and to maintain their status in the eyes of their people. They are a display of conspicuous consumption by the resident chieftain every bit as effective as a brand new Bentley parked in the front drive.

One of the most impressive structures associated with the hillfort was a massive gateway overlooking the roadway leading up to the settlement. At its most sophisticated stage, an architect or specialist builder must have been brought in to oversee the stone and timber construction. The first major phase included the building of a large timber tower with wooden gates. The walls of the gateway contained slots so that massive timber beams could be slid into position to keep the doors firmly closed. This gateway eventually fell into disuse and it was some time before an even more elaborate entrance was built.

This second phase saw the construction of a stone gateway, which was very different from the original entrance. The new one included a large four-post gate tower, incorporating multiple gates rather like a lock in a canal. This allowed the residents to isolate visitors on arrival, thereby giving the guards a chance to check for weapons or hostile intent. In addition to its defensive value, the gateway further increased the status of the chieftain. However, this complex and sophisticated structure subsequently decayed and a variety of timber gate towers were built on the rubble.

The fluctuating history of the gateway at Castell Henllys suggests several possibilities. There might have been periodic shifts of power in the region which created periods when an imposing entrance was not needed; or possibly an elaborate gateway was simply too expensive to maintain in the long term and was allowed to fall into disuse. Another suggestion is that an architect from outside the area supervised the construction but, once he left, the residents did not have the engineering skills to maintain it and so it fell into disrepair.

Relatively few artefacts have been found in the vicinity of the fort, mainly because of the corrosive nature of the acid soil. The most frequent archaeological finds are therefore made from stone or pottery, such as spindle whorls, whetstones and flint flakes from earlier periods. A small hunting spearhead and a sickle blade have also been discovered at Castell Henllys, but iron was such a valuable, high-status commodity that very little was thrown away or lost. However, slag and crucibles have also been found on the site, which suggests that there was some iron and bronze working. Even though Castell Henllys was situated in the extreme west of Iron Age Britain, various non-local artefacts have also been uncovered, including glass beads, pottery and small fragments of bronze. This suggests that the region was visited by neighbouring tribes and might have been part of a much bigger trading network.

Around 100 BC, the occupants of Castell Henllys moved out of the hillfort and settled in a farmstead adjacent to the original site. This might have occurred because there was less of a threat from small-scale conflict, or perhaps because the people needed to grow more food. Whatever the reason, this is a pattern which has been observed in hillforts throughout southern Britain and both scenarios could be a consequence of the political and economic changes resulting from increasing contact with the expanding Roman Empire.

Now, for the first time since 100 BC, the hillfort at Castell Henllys was about to be occupied.

The next morning, the volunteers ate their last breakfast in the twenty-first century and tucked in to what were soon to become forbidden fruits – tomatoes, baked beans, fried potatoes and fresh coffee with sugar, not to mention china plates and cups, forks, tables and chairs. These were only a few of the items that the volunteers would quickly have to learn to live without for the next six and a half weeks. But life in the Iron Age was never totally devoid of choice and many of the elements of a normal English cooked breakfast would have been available to the early Celts, including eggs, bacon, sausages, mushrooms and black pudding. The difference was that in the Iron Age fresh food did not come wrapped in cellophane packs.

The staple carbohydrate for the Iron Age people was bread made from flour ground from spelt wheat and there were a dozen large baskets of spelt grain already stored in the granary awaiting the arrival of the volunteers. The early Celts probably relied on naturally available yeast to make their dough rise, so the bread would have been heavy by modern standards. Iron Age people had no other basic carbohydrate: potatoes were not introduced into Europe from South America until the middle of the sixteenth century AD, rice was not grown in Britain and pasta was not introduced into Italy until the thirteenth century AD.

63

Iron Age vegetables most probably included brassicas such as cabbage or kale, celtic beans, wild parsnips, wild garlic and possibly peas, but did not include tomatoes, carrots, broccoli, cauliflower or sweetcorn. The Iron Age diet also included a wide range of herbs and woodland mushrooms, eaten fresh or dried to keep through the winter. Seasonal fruits were gathered in the woods when they were ripe; they included blackberries, elderberries and crab apples, but nothing exotic – no bananas, grapes, peaches, oranges or pears. Hazelnuts became available in autumn, but not almonds, walnuts, brazil nuts or peanuts. The only sweetener available was honey or fruit.

Autumn was a good time of year for our volunteers to move into the hillfort because the trees and bushes around Castell Henllys were heavy with blackberries, crab apples and hazelnuts. However, Jody was concerned about how they would manage their food under such primitive conditions. 'In modern day life, there's always food around. You always know that you can pop to the shop or there's something in the cupboard. But when you've got to spend hours preparing food, it becomes a major issue. I suppose you've just got to be more careful with it.'

Jody had been a vegetarian, although she decided to eat meat whilst on the hillfort. 'If I was going to eat meat, I'd rather eat something that was free range and that I'd seen being killed. I'd much rather do that than eat factory-produced meat. I don't think I'm going to be putting my hand up to volunteer for killing animals or anything, but I'm comfortable with it.'

Ceris too was happy with the idea of killing animals – at least up to a point. 'As long as there's no suffering and if I don't get too attached to them. I've had lots of pets like ducks and things, and I can't eat duck now. I've hand-raised little duck-lings, and they follow you around and think that you're their mum. And then you see people eating duck and you think, "Oh, but they're so nice!" As long as I don't get too attached, I don't really mind – if I'm hungry.'

The early Celts certainly drank large quantities of alcohol, but it would have been beer rather than wine. Posidonius was quoted by Athenaeus: 'The lower classes drink wheaten beer prepared with honey … drinking a little at a time, taking no more than a mouthful, but they do it rather frequently.' Hops were not used to make beer until the Middle Ages so early Celtic beer would have been based on cereal grains or fermented apples, perhaps sweetened with honey. Mead became a common drink, but probably not until after the arrival of the Romans. Wine too was very popular with the wealthy aristocracy during the Iron Age once

IRON AGE FASHION

Iron Age Britons wore various decorative accessories, including rings, necklaces, bangles and hair clips. Jewellery was often used to fasten clothing and included brooches and pins made from silver or bronze, or occasionally gold. Sometimes the jewellery was decorated with coral. Diodorus Siculus wrote, '… around their wrists and arms they wear bracelets, around their neck necklaces of solid gold, and huge rings they wear as well, and even corselets of gold.'

The aristocracy might also have worn a neck ring called a torc, sometimes made from silver or gold, but often of iron or bronze. Torcs might therefore have indicated a particular rank or status, rather like epaulettes on military uniforms.

To maintain their appearance, the Celts used hair combs made of bone, wood or antler and mirrors made of bronze. The women might well have worn cosmetics (Propertius was critical of Roman women for 'aping the painted Briton') and both sexes carried magic amulets to ward off ghosts, gods and evil spirits.

The latest Iron Age fashion did not stop at clothing and jewellery, for the early Britons also had a penchant for tattooing. Amongst several Roman reports is one from the minor civil servant Herodian who commented that the Britons, whom he refers to as barbarians, 'tattoo their bodies with various patterns and with pictures of all kinds of animals'. Caesar also mentioned tattooing in the *Gallic Wars*: 'The British tattoo themselves with woad (vitrum) which produces a blue colour and gives them a more horrible appearance in battle.'

trade became well established with the Romans. Diodorus Siculus wrote, 'The Gauls are exceedingly addicted to the use of wine … [and the merchants] receive for it an incredible price; for in exchange for a jar of wine they receive a slave.'

Not only would our volunteers have to get used to an Iron Age diet, but they would also have to become accustomed to wearing the clothing of the period. Certainly the highlight of their last morning in the modern world was receiving their costumes. Two complete sets of clothing were given to each of the volunteers, based closely on the type of fabric, cut and colour typical of the period. Everything from the twenty-first century had to go into their empty suitcases – their clothes, watches, money and jewellery. Chris Park even had to give up his penny whistle, which had not left his side for several years. The only exceptions were Laszlo and Rosie's favourite cuddly toys, without which bedtime would never have been quite the same.

◁ The volunteers were asked to leave all their twenty-first possessions behind – with one or two exceptions!

THE WEEK THE COUNTRY RAN DRY

THE EVIDENCE FOR IRON AGE CLOTHING

By all accounts, the early Britons were a spirited and extrovert people, so it is not surprising that the colour and patterns of their clothing should reflect their lively character. The archaeological evidence comes from two main sources. Firstly, clothing preserved in burials gives details about the type of material and the dyes used, as well as the pattern of weaving. For example, the body of a woman was found in the Hulden Fen in Denmark, well preserved in tannic acid. She was wearing a woollen dress in a light and dark brown check. However, in the case of ritual burials, there is no guarantee that these people were interred in their normal clothing.

The second source of evidence comes from the classical texts. For example, Diodorus Siculus described the fashion of the continental Celts thus: 'The clothing they wear is striking – shirts which have been dyed and embroidered in various colours, and breeches, which they call in their tongue *bracae*; and they wear striped cloaks, fastened by a brooch on the shoulder, heavy for winter wear and light in summer, in which are set checks, close together and of varied hues.'

A well-dressed Iron Age male Briton would normally have worn a long outer tunic with an undershirt of thinner material, *braecci* or long trousers, a heavy woollen cloak worn over the shoulders, simple leather sandals strapped over the foot, belts both for the braecci and to go around the tunic and a pouch to carry personal items. Our volunteers also had a second set of lighter clothing which could be worn indoors or as undergarments. Celtic men tended to wear their hair long and sometimes washed it in chalky water to spike it. The men also wore beards or large moustaches. Small bronze razors have been found in archaeological sites and two replicas of these were made for the volunteers, although nobody ever dared to use them!

The Iron Age woman would wear either a long tunic with a full-length skirt, or a peplum (a tubular, sleeveless dress), with a cloak, belt, sandals and a pouch like the men. There is no archaeological or documentary evidence that early Britons wore any underwear so, true to the spirit of the age, underwear was banned from the Castell Henllys site!

△ The volunteers were supplied with two small bronze razors, modelled accurately on Iron Age artefacts.

THE CLASSICAL WRITERS ON THE CELTIC MALE

STRABO: 'The men of Britain are taller than the Gauls and not so yellow-haired. Their bodies are more loosely built. This will give you an idea of their size: I myself in Rome saw youths standing half a foot taller than the tallest in the city although they were bandy-legged and ungainly in build. They live much like the Gauls but some of their customs are more primitive and barbarous.'

STRABO AGAIN: 'They endeavour not to grow fat or pot-bellied, and any young man who exceeds the standard measure of the girdle is punished.'

DIODORUS SICULUS: '... they amass a great amount of gold, which is used for ornament not only by the women but also by the men.'

DIODORUS SICULUS AGAIN: 'The Gauls are tall of body, with rippling muscles, and white skin, and their hair is blond, and not only naturally so, but they also make it their practice by artificial means to increase the distinguishing colour which nature has given them.'

HERODIAN: 'They tattoo their bodies with various patterns and with pictures of all kinds of animals.'

ATHENAEUS: '... though they have very beautiful women, [they] enjoy boys more: so that some of them often have two lovers to sleep with ...'

◁ Bill sports the latest in Iron Age men's fashion: the hand-woven woollen clothing was bright and colourful and a small leather pouch would have held small trinkets, lucky amulets and possibly a knife.

THE CLASSICAL WRITERS ON THE CELTIC FEMALE

AMMIANUS MARCELLINUS (WITH MORE THAN A TOUCH OF EMBELLISHMENT): '… a whole band of foreigners will be unable to cope with one of the [Gauls] in a fight, if he calls in his wife, stronger than he by far and with flashing eyes; least of all when she swells her neck and gnashes her teeth, and poising her huge white arms, begins to rain blows mingled with kicks, like shots discharged by the twisted cords of a catapult.'

DIODORUS SICULUS: 'The woman of the Gauls are not only like men in their great stature but are a match for them in courage as well.'

CASSIUS DIO (ON QUEEN BOUDICA): '… a woman of the British royal family who had uncommon intelligence for a woman … She was very tall and grim; her gaze was penetrating and her voice was harsh; she grew her long auburn hair to the hips and wore a large golden torque and a voluminous patterned cloak with a thick plaid fastened to it.'

JULIUS CAESAR: 'Men have the power of life and death over their wives, as over their children; and when the father of a house has died, his relatives assemble, and if there is anything suspicious about his death they make inquisition of his wives as they would of his slaves …'

▷ Bethan is Welsh and could therefore claim true Celtic ancestry. Here she is wearing a traditional Iron Age peplum, and an iron pendant which she made herself.

The classical writers often commented on the beauty of Celtic women and Ammianus Marcellinus wrote in the fourth century AD: 'But all of them with equal care keep clean and neat, and in those districts, particularly in Aquitania, no man or woman can be seen, be she never so poor, in soiled or ragged clothing …'

Both men and women would probably have had two types of cloak; a light-weight version draped over the shoulders and a heavier version (possibly with a hood), which was warmer and rainproof. The outside of the cloak was probably oiled with lanolin or waxed with tallow to improve its waterproof qualities. The design of their clothing was very straightforward: both the body and the sleeves of the dress or tunic were simple tubes, and consequently the clothes were loose and baggy. The material was sewn together with an inside seam, using needles made from bone, bronze or iron. The one exception was clothing made from leather or skins; here the seam was on the outside, to maintain the waterproof qualities of the hide.

At 11 o'clock, a coach arrived to take the volunteers up to the hillfort and as they drove along the main road they were able to get their first glimpse of what would be their home for the next six and a half weeks. Early September had been unseasonably wet and their walk through the Castell Henllys grounds took them over the Nant Duad, normally little more than a stream, but which could become a torrent after prolonged rainfall. The volunteers passed the herb garden which had been planted ready for their use and which would supplement their extensive supply of dried herbs. On their right, close to the river, was the sullage pit, where they could take a full body wash. Their water supply had been positioned here, close to the river where the original inhabitants of the fort would have collected their water. However, it would take them a good five minutes to walk up the hill to their roundhouses carrying buckets of water, and this was soon to create problems for the volunteers.

As the group emerged from the woodland surrounding the hillfort, they walked past some of the animals which would be their responsibility for the next few weeks. Next to the pig compound (which included two old and very grumpy wild boar/Tamworth-cross pigs) was their latrine, surrounded on two sides by wicker hurdles, which gave only a modicum of privacy. Health regulations meant that we had to provide satisfactory sanitary conditions, and the latrine was a large concrete cesspit sunk into the ground, with a wooden cover over the hole and a simple bench seat above. It was certainly a great improvement on anything the original inhabitants would have used, but it hardly came up to the standards which we have come to expect in the twenty-first century. As Ron Phillips recalls, 'People had started to go quite silent by the time we'd walked past the toilet area … It was the idea of the toilet being so open. I think that shocked everybody. We fully expected something to be not modern, but a little bit more private perhaps, or not stuck on the top of a hill next door to the pigs!'

For Brenda Phillips too, those first few minutes were a bit of a culture shock. 'You've obviously come from a hotel and all the mod cons. It didn't really hit me until I got to the toilet block. I thought, gosh, you know, what have I let myself in for? But if you want to go, you'll go. It was just that it was so open. But we started, I think a couple of days after that, putting ferns on the sides, which did make it a bit more private.'

As they turned the corner on the pathway leading up to the hillfort, they got their first view of what would be home for the next forty-six days. As they walked up to the gateway, the heavens opened and a steady rain began to fall. In their excitement, the volunteers appeared not to notice – which was just as well, because that autumn proved to be the wettest since weather records began.

◁◁ The volunteers were supplied with an authentic set of wooden drinking cups and bowls, wooden spoons, and iron, wood or bone knives.

◁ A wide range of fresh and dried herbs were provided for cooking.

▽ The volunteers enter the hillfort for the very first time, led by Jody, followed by Bethan, Tom, Ceris and Yasmin carrying Rosie.

6

The Reluctant Chieftain

IT WAS AN EXCITING TIME FOR THE GROUP WHEN they finally arrived at the entrance to the hillfort and pushed open the double gates for the first time. This was to be their home for over a month and a half. All the bedding, equipment and stores were laid out in the roundhouses ready for the volunteers to discover for themselves. Chris Park recalls, 'I remember coming, walking up the hill and seeing the antlers on the gate posts and thinking wow! To see the roundhouses and their kind of organic nature is really nice. And to walk into the place and have a look around and see all the kit that we had – all the tools, all the stores of food – you know, the beds and the materials and the clothes … I was really, really pleased.'

In general everyone shared these first impressions. Bethan Jones, who knew a little of what to expect from her time working as an education assistant at an Iron Age site, was more relieved than anything. 'It was much better than I expected! It looks cosy, but then again, you know, we have to live here for seven weeks and I suppose things will gradually change as we go along. But the initial impression was much better than I thought it would be. And I thought it was a beautiful site.'

After the initial euphoria, the group had to settle in quickly. All the roundhouses were checked out for cooking utensils and supplies. Baskets of spelt wheat and bowls of dried herbs were discovered in the granary, and hams and a sheep carcass were found hanging in one of the roundhouses. (See Appendix 1, page 182 for a full list of the provisions.) About three days' worth of ready-prepared food was left for them, so a late lunch of bread and cheese was easy to prepare. But the most important job for that afternoon was to elect a chieftain. They had known each other for only twenty-four hours, so people had to go on first impressions. However, the group had a lot to organize before nightfall and it was important that they had a leader to co-ordinate their efforts.

The group gathered around the fire in the centre of the compound to decide the election process. With no paper or pencils allowed on the site (the original Celts had no written language), some suggested a vote of hands and others a secret ballot with stones being placed in wooden bowls. With everyone talking at once, Chris Park suggested that they should use a 'talking stick' to keep the meeting in order. The idea was that only the person holding the talking stick could speak and it would pass around the group in turn to let everyone have their say. This was a good idea that became very important at later meetings (some of which became very heated), but on this occasion it did not quite catch on as intended. The problem was that not everyone fully understood the concept and some people picked up any small piece of wood left lying around, only to find themselves in verbal competition with the legitimate holder of the talking stick.

It soon became apparent that people were reluctant to put themselves forward for election even if they clearly had designs on the position. During a quiet moment, Yasmin made her feelings clear to Bethan. 'I'd like to put myself forward, but I'd need someone to nominate me. I'm not going to volunteer myself on my own.' Several people felt the same as Yasmin, so it was suggested that only those who positively did *not* want to be chief should raise their hands. This process of elimination left four contenders, as Bethan recalls. 'I knew that Yasmin wanted to be chief. She was very keen. Anne wanted to be chief. David was keen for it, and Chris was willing to be it as well.' Someone pointed out that Chris was a druid and could therefore not be a chieftain (according to the practice of the early Celts), so he stood down and it became a three-way contest. Anne and Chris voted for Dave, Bill voted for his wife Yasmin, and Anne picked up the remaining votes. It was an overwhelming display of confidence in their new chieftain.

Emma Wooster described the general feeling of support for Anne. 'From the start I thought that Anne would be a really good choice of chief. From the outset she was the one that was singing the songs and she seemed to have no inhibitions in that respect – she seemed like a natural performer. It felt like she would be a really good person to front us. I thought it was really nice that we'd chosen a woman because I thought that was quite radical really.'

It was clear that the group did not want a dictatorial leader and elected a mother-figure instead. Ron Phillips summed it up well. 'I don't think anybody wanted to be bossed about and told what to do. They wanted an easy regime, but somebody who would listen and understand and then make her own assumption of what was going on. I think that was Anne's personality right from the word go. She seemed to fit straight into the group and I was certain she would be able to do a chief's job.'

THE SOCIAL ORDER IN THE IRON AGE

Written texts give us a good idea of how Iron Age society was organized, especially in the latter part of the first century BC through to the early part of the first millennium AD. For example, in the second century AD, Ptolemy listed the names of twenty 'tribes' in Ireland and thirty-three in Britain, although the precise numbers varied over time. Each of these tribes was ruled by a leader or chieftain from within a ruling dynasty and an extended family such as this would have lived in a hillfort like Castell Henllys.

Iron Age society had a well-established system of patronage and tribute taxation. The leader might be bound by an oath of allegiance to a higher chieftain or local king. Lower down the tribal pecking order was the noble or warrior class, who swore an oath of allegiance to the local chieftain and would pay a tithe or tax to the leader. The chieftain and nobles might also have owned slaves or 'unfree' workers, perhaps captured during battle. There might also have been a druidic priesthood within a tribe, which would include bards and seers

or diviners. The druids were probably an itinerant class and they alone would have had the freedom to move between the various tribal groups.

The basic social unit of the Iron Age was the extended family, which often spanned as many as four generations. These people were freemen and farmed the land in the immediate vicinity of their farmstead. A freeman would probably be obliged to put his family in a position of 'protective custody' under a member of the warrior class and in return the family would pay a tithe in produce or service to the noble. The tribal aristocracy would also have offered patronage to skilled workers, who included craftsmen such as blacksmiths and bronze-workers as well as teachers, poets, musicians and genealogists.

Within this hierarchical social structure was the facility for decision-making and the tribe would meet during periodic 'fairs' and annual festivals. This was a time when new agreements and alliances were made, marriages arranged, poems recited and general transactions undertaken.

Anne was genuinely surprised by the result of the election and she did harbour private doubts. 'I didn't put forward that I definitely wanted to run, but I said that if everyone thought that I would be a suitable person then I wouldn't refuse … I was flattered and apprehensive – absolutely!'

The choice of a woman as chieftain certainly had parallels with the Iron Age, although Anne would probably not have been very encouraged by the reputation of some of her predecessors (see overleaf). Although the local chieftains were usually male, the elaborate burials of some high-status women suggest that there were

THE CELTIC WARRIOR QUEENS

Both Boudica and Cartimandua became formidable Celtic leaders at a time when some of the Celtic tribes were in rebellion against the invading Roman forces. Boudica (pronounced *boo-dik-a*, and sometimes spelt Boudicca, but not Boadicea) was arguably the most famous Briton of the time. She was queen of the Iceni, a tribe in East Anglia, and she led an uprising against the Romans in AD 61. Together with other Celtic tribes, she led a huge force against the invaders, burning and slaughtering as many as 70,000 Romans and pro-Roman Britons as she sacked Camulodunum (Colchester), Verulamium (St Albans) and the new port of Londinium (London). The Romans reorganized their forces and during their counter-attack, 80,000 Britons are said to have been killed. Defeated, Boudica is thought to have poisoned herself.

Although not as well-known as Boudica, Cartimandua was probably even more powerful as she was queen of the Brigantes, one of the biggest and most powerful tribes in northern Britain. She was married to Venutius and they might have ruled jointly, but Cartimandua was ambitious, scheming and thirsty for power. The Brigantes were closely allied to the Romans, but rivalry developed between Cartimandua and Venutius — no doubt fuelled by the affair which the queen was having with her husband's armour-bearer. Venutius led an open revolt against the pro-Roman group and a Roman legion had to be despatched to quell the uprising and rescue Cartimandua. As Tacitus wrote so succinctly in AD 70; 'The throne was left to Venutius, the war to us.'

△ Anne in party mood, sporting blue woad make-up and her special chieftain's brooch.

occasional female rulers. The documentary evidence of such daunting women as Boudica and Cartimandua also supports the likelihood of tribal 'queens'.

The choice of any leader in a project such as this was bound to be a controversial one and Anne took on a big responsibility trying to organize the group to work effectively and efficiently. Their first job was to decide upon the sleeping arrangements. There were three large roundhouses and one small one, which doubled as the forge. Nik Stanbury, a quiet man, was keen to sleep in the forge by himself. The young people – all seven of them – decided that they wanted to share a house together and they took over the next smallest, which also contained all the supplies for the hillfort. Anne, David and Christopher chose the newly completed chieftain's house where they were joined by Ron and Brenda. That left Bill and Yasmin and their two young children, Laszlo and Rosie, with the second largest house to themselves. The choice of living arrangements proved to be a critical factor in the way the group dynamics developed over the next few weeks.

Once the sleeping arrangements were sorted out, the group had to be instructed in the care of the livestock, and in particular they had to learn how to milk the goats and the Dexter cows. Chris Park had lived as a goat herder in southern France and soon developed a close attachment to the goats, while Emma and Bethan were also keen to learn how to milk the animals. The cows were less of a success. As they were being brought into their overnight compound, they took fright at the sight of the two Tamworth pigs and one of the cows and her calf ran off down the lane. They were eventually found over an hour later in the nearby village.

△ Chris Park developed a close relationship with Diamond and Jock, the two goats.

The animals provided for the volunteers were based as closely as possible on archaeological evidence, mainly from excavated bones. Unfortunately, bone evidence is often fraught with problems; they were boiled or roasted before being thrown away or sometimes used as tools; dogs chewed them or pigs completely destroyed them. Afterwards, they became covered for 2000 years, often in acid soils, before being excavated as archaeological evidence.

▷ The ring beam was an essential structural part of the roof, distributing the lateral thrust of the roof evenly to the rafters and then to the ground. Once the roof timbers and ring beam were securely attached, the whole structure became very stable.

THE IRON AGE ROUNDHOUSE

After more than 2000 years of weathering and decay, little archaeological evidence of Iron Age housing survives apart from a handful of post-holes and wall-slots. Identifying the pattern of construction is complicated, because over hundreds of years buildings were rebuilt on the same site, and in southern England storage pits were dug and abandoned in the same area. This can leave an Iron Age site peppered with a confusing and conflicting mass of evidence. On the Danebury site alone, it has been estimated that approximately

△ Although most roundhouses were probably built with walls made from wattle and daub, some houses were built with walls made from vertical timber planks set in a circular wall-slot.

4,500 storage pits and 18,000 post-holes were sunk over a period of 450 years (see page 18).

Apart from post-hole evidence, Iron Age sites also reveal fragments of daub used to plaster walls, and channels created by wooden walls. From this evidence it has been possible to build experimental reconstructions of Iron Age dwellings, although we cannot be sure that they are exactly the same as the originals.

The roof was the most complicated part of the structure, but inevitably it leaves no evidence in the archaeological record. It seems that usually between four and six main rafters were leant against the top of a central pole and lashed together at the apex. A pointed, circular roof cannot accommodate more than a few beams coming together at the top, so a ring beam had to be fixed about 1.5 metres (5ft) below the top of the roof. The ring beam ran right around the upper roof and secondary rafters were attached to it, stopping just short of the apex (see picture, above right).

Coppiced hazel purlins were then attached to the rafters with wooden pegs, which further strengthened the structure and provided support for the tight bundles of thatch which were tied or 'sewn' to the hazel supports and overlapped to make a waterproof covering. Once complete, the roof had to withstand several tonnes of timber and thatch.

The walls of a roundhouse were usually made from wattle, woven from thin hazel branches about 1–3cm (about 1in) in diameter. The wattle was

then daubed, which further reinforced the structure. The final construction created a spacious, warm dwelling, typically 5–15 metres (15–50ft) in diameter and 5–8 metres (15–27ft) high. The aerodynamic shape of a roundhouse meant that there was never a flat surface facing the weather and modern reconstructions have withstood hurricane-force winds.

BUILDING MATERIALS

The building materials used for Iron Age houses were obtained locally and required the sophisticated management of woodland. Oak was the most favoured timber for posts and rafters because of its durability. Complete trunks as big as 40cm (16in) in diameter were used as the main structural supports for roundhouses and cleft (split) timber would be used for door-frames and wall-planks. Timber was cleft using iron or hardwood wedges and it was a relatively quick and effective technique to split timbers to make planks. Cleft wood also had the advantage that the natural break was less likely to rot than a sawn surface. Rot, especially where the timbers were set in the ground, was probably the most common reason why a roundhouse had to be abandoned or rebuilt.

Walls were occasionally made from wooden planks, or more likely were plastered in the mixture of clay, straw, dung, animal hair and sometimes blood which was used to make up daub. Daubing required two people working on opposite sides of the wattle. The daub was pushed through from each side and smoothed off; when dry, it made a tough, waterproof wall, but required regular patching. However, wattle and daub was a very versatile combination that was also used to build furnaces and bread ovens.

The branches used in the walls and roof were grown by coppicing – a technique whereby the main trunk of the tree is cut and the stump or stool then sends up numerous shoots. The most common trees used for coppicing were hazel or willow. It usually took about seven years for the branches to reach the correct length and thickness. The early Britons must therefore have developed an effective system of woodland management in order to guarantee a regular supply of material.

Roofs were thatched either with straw left over from the autumn harvest or more likely with river reed, which was more durable and waterproof.

▷ The rafters overlap the outside wall of a roundhouse by up to a metre (3ft), which allowed the rain to run off the roof, away from the walls.

Nevertheless, bones are commonly found in excavations and can reveal a great deal of information. For example, during the first ten years of the excavation of the Danebury hillfort in Hampshire nearly 250,000 individual bone fragments were recovered. Each piece had to be washed, marked, measured and identified, and notes made of any evidence of butchery or disease. From bone fragment evidence such as this we can learn much about domesticated animals during the Iron Age.

The breed of cattle used in the Iron Age has been identified as the extinct shorthorn (*bos longiftons*), a small animal compared to most modern breeds. The nearest equivalent animals today are the Welsh Black, the Kerry of Ireland and the medium-legged Dexter (which is descended from the Kerry). The Dexter is a small, docile animal, which is still bred today for both milk and meat. The original Iron Age shorthorn would also have been an important source of meat, milk and dairy products for the early Britons, and so our volunteers were given two Dexter cows for milking and a steer for slaughter.

Despite its small stature, the Iron Age shorthorn would have been a powerful animal and a pair yoked together and pulling an ard could work a hectare (2.5 acres) of land or more in a couple of days. Cattle were also used as a ready form of wealth which could be displayed, traded or invested, and it is likely that the cattle-owning aristocracy lent their animals to freemen farmers in return for goods and services.

Sheep were also common during the Iron Age, providing an essential source of wool for clothing and possibly milk. They generally seem to have been butchered at

▽ David and Anne feeding the Soay sheep. Because the volunteers did not start the project until September, they were provided with hay and commercial animal feed.

an old age; therefore the animals were probably not reared primarily for meat. Preserved bone and wool from Iron Age sites suggest that these sheep were small and very similar to the Soay, a breed which has survived virtually unaltered for two thousand years on the island of St Kilda off the west coast of Scotland. Both rams and ewes have horns, long legs, and are often mistaken for goats. They are also capable of jumping fences 2 metres (6.5ft) high and cannot be controlled by dogs. Their meat is remarkably fat-free and tastes rather like venison. The wool is short and was probably plucked off the animal using bone combs before being spun into yarn and woven. Our volunteers were given a small flock of Soays and the rams were available to them for slaughter.

Goats were also kept by Iron Age farmers, but as they were very similar to sheep, the bones are difficult to tell apart unless the anklebone or skull is found. The direct descendant of the Iron Age animal is probably the rare Old English Goat,

WILD ANIMALS DURING THE IRON AGE

Many parts of Britain look little different today from how they must have done in the Iron Age, but many animals have become extinct and others have been introduced from abroad. Red and roe deer were more widespread during the Iron Age than today, and wolves, bears and wild boar no longer roam the forests of Britain as they did then.

Many of our common rodents were not found in Britain during the Iron Age. The black rat did not arrive from the Middle East until the twelfth and thirteenth centuries, bringing with it the Black Death which wrought havoc throughout Europe. The brown rat was a later immigrant and the grey squirrel arrived later still, having been introduced from North America. Rabbits, too, were late arrivals, probably brought by the Normans from southern Europe for the cooking pot, although hares were already established in pre-Roman Britain.

The early Britons, however, still had their rodent problems – the bones of yellow-necked and house mice have been found in grain stores. Bones of the short-tailed and water vole, badgers, foxes, moles and weasels have also been found in Iron Age sites.

which is small and tough. However, like all goats, it is capable of eating almost anything and this is not always an advantage on a farm. For this reason, there were probably many fewer goats than sheep in an Iron Age settlement.

The Iron Age people also kept domestic pigs and hunted for wild boar. The domestic pig from the pre-Roman period is now extinct and the nearest modern equivalent is probably the Tamworth crossed with wild boar, like the pigs at Castell Henllys. The European wild boar is still hunted on the continent, but it no longer survives in the wild in Britain. Pigs were useful animals to have around during the Iron Age. They could live almost anywhere and would feed off all manner of waste. They could be turned out into fields to root in the stubble and would leave good quality manure behind. They could also be left to forage in woodland during the winter when food was short. They were prolific breeders and the meat was delicious, so it is little surprise that the archaeological record contains many figurines of pigs and wild boar, suggesting that Iron Age people held the animal in high regard.

Horse bones, especially the skull, are commonly found in Iron Age sites. Horses were not kept as farm animals but were considered a status symbol. Julius Caesar described how the Iron Age warriors rode into battle in a chariot drawn by two horses, and he himself faced this onslaught on two occasions when he fought the Britons in southern England in 55 and 54 BC. Horse bones from some sites show signs of having been subjected to butchery. This suggests that when a horse reached the end of its useful life it might have been killed for food, either for humans, dogs or pigs. The Iron Age horse was small, tough and fast (really a pony, not more than 10–11 hands high) and the nearest modern equivalent is probably the Exmoor pony.

Dogs and cats existed in Iron Age settlements as well. The Greek historian and geographer Strabo listed hunting dogs as a British export. '[Britain] produces corn, cattle, gold, silver and iron. These things are exported along with hides, slaves and dogs suitable for hunting.' Cat bones have also been found and cats might have been useful in keeping vermin in check. Bees, both wild and almost certainly domesticated, provided honey as an essential source of sweetening. Beeswax was also used for *cire perdue* (lost wax) metal casting. River, lake and sea fish offered a change of diet whenever they could be caught.

△ Little Chris proved to be the most successful egg-collector and on one occasion found over a dozen in one place.

Iron Age farmers also kept domestic fowl, but bird bones are small and hollow and do not survive well in the archaeological record, so the evidence is sparse. Their chickens were probably similar to the Indian Red Jungle Fowl and the Old English Game Fowl. Both of these are now rare breeds and are poor egg-layers compared with modern birds. The volunteers at Castell Henllys were provided with Old English Game Fowl as well as modern varieties as egg-layers. Bone analysis suggests that the early Britons also kept geese and ducks and so our volunteers were given two male geese, mainly as an early warning against prowling foxes. The two geese were inseparable during their stay at Castell Henllys and, being devoid of any female company, they soon became known as Gordon and Guy the gay geese.

Vegetables were an essential source of vitamin C for the early Britons, but there was little choice. Fat Hen, sometimes called melde, tastes a bit like spinach when young and is thought to have been the main green vegetable in Britain until the introduction of cabbage. (We supplied our volunteers with unlimited quantities of kale, which is a fair substitute.) Fat Hen was grown for both human and animal consumption and had the big advantage that it matured in a little

▽ Emma on cooking duty, preparing the much maligned kale. The volunteers were so desperate to find new ways of cooking the vegetable that they even resorted to kale and goats' cheese pizza!

over three months. Wild mustard and charnock both taste rather like cabbage, and wild parsnips were grown as a root crop (and are still found growing around Iron Age sites).

The Celtic bean was a nutritious and common staple for the Iron Age people and it also had the advantage of a nitrogen nodule in its root system, making it ideal for rotation with cereal crops. Flax was a versatile crop; its leaves were used for animal fodder and linen could be obtained from the stalks by a process called retting. Stacks of the plant can be soaked in water for approximately ten days to allow bacteria to break down the vegetable matter; the plant is then crushed, soaked again and combed out over spikes to extract the linen thread. Oil can also be extracted from the crushed seeds of flax. Gold of Pleasure was another source of oil and the plant could also be eaten. It is likely that many weeds were eaten as well and the new leaves of many wild plants are often quite palatable. Finally, various nuts, fruits and fungi would have been available in the woods and forests from summer through to autumn, and the Iron Age people would certainly have picked what they could to vary their diet.

The early Celts clearly had an adequate supply of meat, fish, milk, cheese and vegetables, although the choice was limited and often seasonal. The animals provided a stock of leather, skins, fur, rawhide rope, horn, feathers (for adornment and arrows), bone, antlers, wool and manure to fertilize the ground. The Iron Age people were able to exploit their natural environment and use a diversity of natural resources which differed little from those enjoyed by people living in early medieval Britain, over a thousand years later.

The main challenge facing our volunteers was whether they could master enough of these Iron Age skills in seven weeks to survive. Chris had lived as a goat herder in France, so he was able to teach others how to milk and manage the goats. Anne and David volunteered to look after the two Dexter cows and their calves, but milking them proved to be much more difficult than the goats. After her first attempt, Anne was not very impressed with the results. 'I got about a dessert-spoonful of milk. I could probably spend the next seven weeks getting enough for a cup of tea!' As it turned out, the goats provided so much milk that the art of milking the Dexters never had to be mastered, and the cows were left in peace with their calves.

The volunteers still had to face killing chickens and butchering the rams later in the week, but for the moment at least they were tired but warm and they still had enough food to last them for two more days. Even the steady drizzle which had set in during that first afternoon did little to dampen their spirits. Anne especially was feeling good about the day and her election as chieftain. 'My goodness, what a day it's been! A fantastic day. A very long day. For reasons known only unto them, they chose me as the chief and I'm just so thrilled, I can't believe my luck. I hope I'll be a good chief. I'll try very hard.'

As it turned out, she was very soon to be put to the test.

◁ Jody and Mark became experts at grinding corn. Jody is using a saddle quernstone and Mark a rotary quernstone.
▽ Anne used one of the precious hides spread out on the earth floor to catch the flour. The grain is poured into the central hole in the upper stone; this is laboriously rotated to grind the wheat into coarse flour, which gradually spills out between the two stones.

7
Norming and Storming

THE NEXT MORNING THERE WAS a very different feeling on the hillfort. Smoke was rising gently from the thatch of the roundhouses, so the fires had kept burning during the night. The film crew arrived early, expecting the volunteers to be making the most of the good weather and the early sunshine. Instead, Gordon and Guy the gay geese had the hillfort to themselves. Anne was the first to emerge, looking tired. Like most of the volunteers, she had not slept well on a strange bed during that first night. 'I think it says quite a lot about what we're used to at home. We're used to central heating, we're used to certain levels of comfort and our bodies are just going to have to adjust. And my body hasn't adjusted yet, but we'll get there!' Most people found themselves cold during the night and Brenda complained that she found her hay mattress uncomfortable and could not move the lumps around into a better position.

Unfortunately, both Laszlo and Rosie Billinghurst were ill during the night as a result of drinking too much rich goat's milk. They had kept their mother up for most of the night and by the afternoon Yasmin was close to tears from a combination of lack of sleep and nicotine deprivation. 'It was awful, and it doesn't help that I've had to give up smoking. That's really, really hard. That's all it is. I mean, I'm so glad I'm crying rather than punching people in the face. You'll probably see me cry a lot more over the next few weeks, because it's been twenty years – twenty years of smoking!'

Slowly that first morning, the group began to organize themselves. Encouraged by the warm weather, people went off to collect berries and hazelnuts in the surrounding woodland before the squirrels got there first. There was enough bread on site for a couple of days and enough flour for a little longer, but it would not last for long, so Mark, Jody and

△ Yasmin gave up smoking when she joined the project, which made her first few days more of a trial than most. She later confessed to smuggling cigarettes onto the site.

Anne took turns on the unfamiliar quernstones to grind the spelt grain into flour. In fact, the grinding of the spelt wheat was one of the big successes of the project. The BBC had provided three rotary quernstones and a saddle quernstone, expecting that as many as three people would have to work for several hours a day to grind enough flour for the group's needs. In fact, they were so efficient that one person could grind enough flour for the day in just a few hours.

The group were also given instructions on how to make 'honey beer'. Their brewing instructions were based on an early medieval recipe for cyser, a traditional honey-flavoured cider similar to the type of alcoholic drink the Iron Age people would have made. The beer was the first of several 'time challenges' which they were to receive, which gave them details of how to master various tasks which were essential to survival in the Iron Age.

These were still very early days for the group and people were still getting to know each other. Psychologists popularly refer to this as the 'norming' stage, when people are polite and still finding their way socially. 'Everybody was kind of skirting around each other in a very nice way,' recalls Emma. 'Of course, people didn't know each other's true characters, so it was a bit like cocktail party talk really for the first few days – very polite, very reserved, very considerate of each other. Not much time for all our annoying habits to come out.'

There were, however, urgent tasks to attend to. Meals had to be arranged, and the group found that cooking three times a day on an open fire in primitive conditions was very time-consuming. The cooking also used up a vast amount of firewood which had to be collected from their supply at the bottom of the hillfort. Bill found that the oven in his roundhouse had a crack in it, which had to be repaired with daub before it would get up to cooking temperature. Not all of the iron knives had been provided with handles, so Nik, Ron and Brenda took over responsibility for fitting wooden and antler handles to the iron blades.

△ Nik attaches wooden handles to the iron knife blades by heating the blade white hot and forcing the handle onto the hot metal.

HONEY BEER

To make 2 gallons of cyser, take 8 pounds of apples and 3 pounds of honey.

Mash the apples in a bucket and add the honey and 2 gallons of water warmed to blood temperature. You can also add some blackberries for good measure if you wish — the fruit adds body, taste and natural yeast for fermentation. But don't try any other fruit.

Cover the bucket tightly with a cloth and after about a week, listen carefully. If the fizzing noise has stopped, the fermentation is nearly complete. Try the beer for taste.

Strain the liquid into a barrel and allow the fermentation to continue — the longer this lasts, the stronger the beer, so be careful!

You can now start on another brew, and add this to the barrel once fermentation is complete.

However, the biggest problems the volunteers faced were caused by some leaky buckets and cauldrons. The wooden buckets were new and some of them would not hold water because they needed soaking in the river for twenty-four hours to swell and stop the leaks. This made it very frustrating on the first day to fill the main wooden water barrel used for storage up on the hillfort. By the time people had walked the five minutes up from the tap near the river, half the water had leaked or spilled out of the bucket. To compound the problem, one of the new metal cooking cauldrons was also leaking and this made it difficult to boil large quantities of water. The Iron Age forge was not yet functioning and the volunteers could not mend the cauldron for themselves, so it was returned to the local twenty-first-century blacksmith for repair – and an extra few smaller ones were ordered for good measure.

Anne was trying to organize the group to best effect and asked for an inventory to be made of everything in the hillfort. Unfortunately many of the smaller items such as bronze needles, knives and bowls were lost in the gloom of the dark roundhouses during the first few days.

On the Tuesday, their second full day on the hillfort, the volunteers were given their next 'time challenge' – instructions on how to make charcoal, which was an essential skill to master in the Iron Age. Burning charcoal is probably the oldest chemical process known to man and the technique goes back to around 2000 BC in Britain, and much earlier in some other places. It is possible to smelt certain metal ores by using wood fires alone, but to make bronze and iron the high temperatures reached in a charcoal fire are essential. Without charcoal, the technological evolution into the Bronze and Iron Ages simply could not have happened.

Mark, Tom, Nik and young Christopher began to build a charcoal clamp that morning, following techniques which were used during the Iron Age. A large clamp could take days or even weeks to fire, but a small clamp a little over one metre (3ft) in diameter could be finished in about twenty-four hours.

First, Tom marked out a circle which defined the size of the clamp, and then timber was stacked to make a narrow, central chimney. (Sometimes a length of timber called a 'motty peg' could be positioned vertically in the centre, and then removed at the final stage, as an alternative way of making a central hole.) Then equal-sized lengths of timber were stood vertically around the central stack to build up a dome-shaped mound. The timber was about 40cm (16in) long with a diameter

▽ Having the water tap sited by the river at the bottom of the hill proved to be too much effort for the volunteers. After a week, the mains tap was relocated close to the roundhouses.

CHARCOAL

Charcoal was an important commodity during the Iron Age. Without it you will not be able to smelt iron. So the time has come to select your charcoal-making team to begin their task tomorrow.

Be aware that it can take several days to make charcoal and constant vigilance is essential if you are going to be successful. Your people will need food and must spend a night out in the open.

Your charcoal-makers must find a suitable site at least 4ft in diameter, close to a source of water. Rabbit tunnels and mole runs must be blocked if they are within the area of the clamp.

Cut one cubic yard of dry, seasoned round wood 14–18 inches long and 2–3 inches thick. Oak, birch, ash and hazel are suitable, but alder is best for iron smelting because it burns hot.

Cut one cubic yard of turf with at least 2 inches of soil attached, and dig half a cubic yard of loose soil. Cut bracken, fern, grass or other vegetation to cover the clamp. You must also have a section of hurdle to hand to use as a windbreak.

This is an important challenge, but you can take heart. Your slaves have left a supply of charcoal at the bottom of the hillfort for your immediate use. There you will also find wood cut to size from which you can make your charcoal. Do not burn this wood on your fire — it will be much more valuable to you as charcoal.

∇ Mark and Tom keep watch over the completed charcoal clamp. If the earth seal is breached, oxygen will destroy the charcoal-making process.

of 5–7cm (2–3in), and was tightly packed leaving the minimum space between each piece of wood. The mound of timber was then covered with a thick layer of damp leaves and bracken, then with turf and a layer of soil. (If a motty peg had been used, this is the stage at which it would have been removed, leaving a hole running down the very centre of the timber stack.) The finished structure was a useable charcoal clamp.

Nik then brought hot embers down from the hillfort in a metal cauldron and used them to start a wood fire. Once the fire was well established, glowing embers were carefully poured down into the central hole in the clamp. This set fire to the logs at the base of the clamp and, once there was a strong fire burning inside with flames clearly visible coming out of the top, the central hole was covered with turf and soil, or 'capped off'. This immediately cut off the supply of oxygen to the flames burning inside. The fire continued to burn, but instead of using oxygen it was consuming the natural gases in the wood. This oxygen-free environment is essential to the charcoal-burning process and is called a reducing atmosphere.

A constant watch had to be kept over the clamp, because as wood turns to charcoal it shrinks, and the clamp could collapse on itself. If cracks were to appear

in the soil covering the clamp, oxygen would get to the fire and destroy the process. Conversely, if the fire inside the clamp had seemed to be dying out, then small holes would have needed to be poked into the base of the clamp to get the combustion process going. So Mark and Tom built a rudimentary shelter next to the clamp and settled down for the night to keep watch. Unfortunately, it began to rain that evening and the two apprentice charcoal-makers were soaked. Tom remembers it well. 'It was about one o'clock or something in the morning and it was pissing down with rain. Which wasn't very pleasant. It was coming straight through our roof.' Mark and Tom packed up for the night and went back to the comfort of the roundhouse. When they uncovered the clamp the following morning, they found that the fire had gone out and the charcoal-making effort was only a partial success.

If the process had gone according to plan, the gases in the timber would have been slowly burnt off to leave carbonized wood (charcoal). When this stage is complete, the hot charcoal is still liable to spontaneously burst into flames because of the heat, so the clamp must be slowly doused with water to cool it down. Charcoal-making requires skill and experience and for thousands of years it has been a full-time job. It is also a very time-consuming process, especially if you have to cut your own timber. It takes between three and four tonnes of wood to make a tonne of charcoal – but without charcoal, the mastery of iron would never have been achieved.

The day the charcoal-makers were at work, the chickens arrived. David Rickard kept chickens at home, so an expert checked that he knew how to kill them quickly and humanely by breaking their necks. Unfortunately, at his first attempt, Dave pulled the head completely off the bird. But, together with Ceris Williams, he gamely gutted and plucked the chickens for the evening meal.

Meanwhile, the day arrived for the group to face the slaughter of the rams. Twenty-first-century people are as far removed from butchering animals as it is possible to get and the nearest most of us get to preparing meat for consumption is to open a cellophane packet from the supermarket and trim a little fat off before cooking. Ever since the BSE crisis in Britain, the slaughter of domestic livestock has been strictly governed by new regulations drawn up by the Ministry of Agriculture, Fisheries and Food. These require a professional slaughterman to kill the animal and prepare it for butchering. What is officially referred to as 'Specified Risk Material'

▽ David and Ceris volunteered to prepare the first batch
of chickens for supper. They saved the feathers for a pillow,
but left out the entrails – which were soon cleared up by foxes.

must also be removed for safe disposal: SRM varies according to the animal, but generally includes the head, the spleen and the spinal cord. So thanks to MAFF regulations and the dexterity of Andrew from the abattoir, the volunteers were spared the actual job of killing the two young rams, but they did stand by to watch the deadly deed. Chris then took over the responsibility for butchering the carcasses, curing the skins and preparing the intestines to stuff to make sausages.

Like all traditional farmers, the Iron Age Britons were responsible for their animals from conception to consumption; their very survival depended on a regular supply of good quality meat. If the animals did not flourish, then neither did their owners. But these animals supplied the Iron Age farmer with much more than protein. They provided hides and wool for footwear and clothing, bones for broth and tools, fat for cooking and candles, gut for rope, intestines for sausage skins, and rennet, an essential ingredient for making hard cheese found in the stomach of an immature calf.

Nobody can be certain how the Iron Age Britons slaughtered their animals but, in a violent and uncertain world, the technique is unlikely to have been compassionate; animal rights were still a long way off in pre-Roman Britain. However, once killed, the carcass needed to be quickly drained of blood. The simplest technique would have been to tie a rope around the rear legs of the animal, cut its throat and hang it from the branch of a tree. Nothing would have been wasted from such a valuable resource. The blood would have been collected in a bucket and used to make black pudding, perhaps mixed with herbs and wild garlic before being stuffed into the bladder or intestine.

Once Chris had skinned the carcass, he scraped the hide free of any fat and flesh and put it aside, ready for curing. The volunteers were going to eat the meat almost immediately, but during the Iron Age the Celts would have used a variety of techniques to preserve it: it could be smoked, dried in the sun, packed with salt or put in a barrel of brine. All of these techniques were necessary ways of preserving meat for the winter. The bones would be picked free of marrow and boiled to make stock before being used to make picks, fishhooks, knives, combs, needles and any number of other useful household tools.

Skins and hides were important by-products of domesticated animals for the Iron Age people. We cannot be exactly sure what techniques they used, but preserving hides and furs is a very old art and many successful methods have been developed over the years. Hides and skins deteriorate quickly so unless they are tanned immediately they must be treated or cured with salt. This is the technique Chris Park used on his sheepskins. He laid the hide out hair side down and sprinkled it with fresh, clean salt, rubbing it in well. Curing removes moisture from the skin, prevents spoilage and discourages flies. The salting can be repeated after a few days if the first application becomes saturated with moisture.

The process of tanning turns a skin or hide into leather, either by soaking or by rubbing with a tanning agent. First, the skin must be softened and thoroughly cleaned so it is free of flesh and grease. Water will also soften the skin if it has been cured. A very old tanning technique, possibly used in the late Iron Age, was to soak the skin in a mixture of salt and alum. This produces skins which are flexible and stretchable. Native Americans used wood ash to remove the hair from the skin and rubbed the brains of the animal into the skin as a tanning agent. The early Britons might also have used this technique, and it is said that every mammal has sufficient brain to cure its own skin. Native American women also chewed the hides to produce a soft buckskin.

△ Big Chris stretched out the skin from one of the slaughtered rams over a wooden frame to cure.

That afternoon, Bill was on cooking duty and it fell to him to cook the chickens that David had slaughtered earlier in the day. However, the volunteers were finding it difficult to keep up with the demands of making three meals a day and mealtimes were getting later and later. Cooking for supper that evening started late in the afternoon and it was dark before the chickens were ready. Unable to see what they were eating, some of the volunteers probably ate partially cooked chicken, which was to have disastrous consequences.

Meanwhile, the following morning the volunteers continued the labour of carrying fuel and water up to the hillfort. Nik in particular worked hard filling the main water barrel. Unfortunately, after he had made several trips up the hill, somebody decided to relocate the container in a different place and poured the water out

▽ Bill on cooking duty the night before the food poisoning. The meal was not ready until after dark and people were not aware they could be eating partly-cooked chicken – with disastrous consequences!

in order to move it more easily. Nik came back to find all his hard work was for nothing. It was a devastating blow, as he had not only worked hard getting water up to the site, but had spent the previous day cutting turf for the charcoal clamp.

Nik had eaten little for breakfast that morning, and the combination of insufficient food and over-exertion caused him to turn giddy and pass out. This coincided with Bill becoming very ill, having probably eaten undercooked chicken the previous night. Five days into the project the local doctor was called for an emergency visit. Fortunately neither illness was serious. Bill was prescribed oral rehydration salts and Nik was given glucose and a honey pancake to get his blood sugar level back to normal. The episode shook everybody on site, as Emma recalled. 'When Nick went down it really frightened everybody. I think that we got to a crisis point really. I mean, looking back now, it just seems so ridiculous that we got into that situation in the first place. I don't know how it happened … you can't see the wood for the trees at all. It's just that you've got no perspective, especially if you're living completely out of the situation that you would normally.'

It was becoming clear that some concessions had to be made to the twenty-first century if the volunteers were to remain healthy. They had found it difficult to get an organized system in place; for example, they were eating late in the afternoon, which meant that it was dark when they wanted to wash up. Their wooden bowls and eating utensils were now very dirty and tummy bugs could easily spread in these conditions. Ron and Brenda had learnt from their extensive camping experience and kept their eating utensils to themselves. They tried to pass on their knowledge to others, but without success. 'It's really annoying when you tell people to do these sorts of things, to wash properly and eat plenty of honey, to replace body fluids, and they don't do it. And of course there's a great need to drink a lot of water. You can survive on water and honey but not on water alone. You need quite a few nutrients to get you by.'

Throughout the project, Ron and Brenda religiously took a spoonful of honey a day and kept their utensils clean – and they never had a day's illness. 'Three days into it, I saw we were going to have problems,' recalls Ron. 'It looked that way anyway, because we were using buckets for all sorts of different things. We designated a bucket for the water barrel, but people were putting the bucket on the floor and then dipping it back into the barrel, and so contaminating the water in the barrel.'

'First of all we didn't even think to have our own cup and bowl,' Emma remembers, 'and then we had at least twenty-four discussions about whether we should keep our bowls or whether the bowls should be washed every night by someone else. So it just seemed the most basic organizational things were very difficult, because everyone was being terribly nice. Nobody wanted to say, "No I think that's a really bad idea." Nobody really wanted to confront anybody in that way … I think that's why things went wrong. I think that, even though we didn't want a dictatorial chief, in the first few days, it would actually have been really good for someone to stand there and say right we're doing this – this – this!'

The volunteers had been advised about keeping their utensils clean during their safety briefing and they were now reminded of it. They had experimented with salt, sand and wood ash (which is caustic) to clean their bowls but, as a precautionary measure, washing-up detergent was now brought on to the site, together with pan scourers and sponges. Finally, to cheer up flagging spirits, more fresh food was brought up to the site so that nobody had to cook that night.

On the Saturday morning, Nik Stanbury decided to leave the project after only six days at the hillfort. He was still not feeling well after his collapse two days previously and he had never felt comfortable being under the constant scrutiny of the cameras. He had also had word from home that there were problems with the lease on his business premises which needed to be sorted out. People were sorry to see him leave, in particular Bill and Yasmin, who had struck up a close friendship with him during their few days together. The volunteers had been chosen with a careful balance of abilities and the group was going to miss Nik's strength and willingness to put in more than his fair share of the hard labour.

Ceris Williams also left the site the same day, albeit for very different reasons. During the night she had developed a sore throat and swollen glands. She was taken to the local surgery in the morning and the doctor was concerned that it could be the early stages of meningitis. Ceris was then taken immediately to the local hospital, where tests confirmed the infection was nothing more serious than tonsillitis. However, it was another indication of how vulnerable twenty-first-century people have become to infections and how much we now rely on swift medical intervention. Ceris was prescribed antibiotics and stayed in a cottage nearby for a week until she had made a full recovery and could return to the hillfort.

This weekend (just one week into the project) also coincided with the end of the 'norming' stage and the start of a period of 'storming'. Strong friendships were

▽ Rosie and Laszlo found the Iron Age village a playground without limits.

being made, especially amongst the younger people in the small roundhouse. But tensions were also developing between some of the older people, and between Yasmin and Anne in particular. Anne was finding the role of chieftain a challenge and had little experience of organizing a large group. Yasmin too was having a difficult time trying to cope with two young children, who were now fully recovered from their tummy trouble and were as boisterous and energetic as ever – and she was still suffering from nicotine withdrawal. 'I don't feel I've done anything. I just feel completely useless. And the fire's gone out now as well, which doesn't help. So today I'm going to knit bedsocks for everybody, and then I'll feel I've done something positive. And I won't feel like going home and crying all day!'

A combination of lack of sleep, the culture shock of being thrust into an alien environment, and having to cope with the additional pressures of leadership and children brought the two women into open confrontation. Like so many arguments, problems had built up over misunderstandings and minor irritations were allowed to grow out of proportion. Yasmin was also becoming very frustrated with what she saw as a lack of organization and leadership in the group. 'We've been here over three days now and we are still completely disorganized. This is a camp and it should be run, in my opinion, like a military camp. You should have tasks that you know you're doing – you're responsible for this, you have to do it!'

The confrontation came to a head on the Sunday morning, exactly one week into the project. It had been decided by the group that the tensions between the two women needed to be discussed openly. Yasmin arrived late at the meeting, made a statement of apology to the group and took full responsibility for her behaviour. She then got up and walked out of the meeting without any further discussion. Both Anne and David were now even more confused about the problem than ever. David was in the process of talking about the breakdown in the relationship when Bill flew into a rage over something that he had said about Yasmin which Bill thought was unjust. Harsh words were said that were difficult to retract.

The conflict had now escalated to include the two husbands. The meeting, inevitably, came to an end in acrimony and Anne broke down in tears. Clearly, things could not continue unresolved after this very public confrontation. The group asked Chris Park to mediate between the two couples, but he felt that this put him in an impossible position since he was living twenty-four hours a day with the four individuals concerned. So Chris turned to Peter Firstbrook, the series producer, who was present at the meeting, and asked if he would take over the responsibility of mediating between the couples. It was a difficult time for everyone involved. Both couples wanted to stay on the project, yet that was unrealistic unless they could come to terms with the antagonism that had grown up between them. Unless the issue was resolved, it would jeopardize the whole project.

Peter asked both parties to have a two-hour cooling-off period before returning for a mediation session. Both couples asked for the discussion not to be filmed. Bill spoke first and apologized for his behaviour at the group meeting. Others spoke in turn through Peter, who was acting as mediator. Chris's 'talking stick' was used to good effect and everything was controlled and polite, if a little chilly. There was a genuine attempt by all parties to find reconciliation and everyone was prepared to accept some responsibility for the problem.

The outcome was an understanding that the situation created by the project was an artificial one and that the group had not come together through a process of mutual selection. Therefore it was not surprising – in fact it was to be expected – that some people would not get on as well as others. But everybody wanted to stay on the project, so a solution had to be found to handle the situation. Individuals agreed not to jump to hasty conclusions, to be aware that small misunderstandings could easily get out of hand, and to recognize that expressions and intonations could easily be misinterpreted. Both couples knew they could never become friends, but there was a sincere determination on the part of everybody concerned to be more tolerant and to make the best of an uncomfortable situation, as Emma recalls. 'The frostiness remained. The thing is, I'm privy to a lot more information than most because I'm interviewing people and asking them questions that you probably would not do in a normal conversation … I talked to Yasmin about it and she says, "I'll never be Anne's best friend, but we've come to a solution," and I was happy with that … I think everybody accepted that it was the best situation we were going to come to.'

It had been a testing first week for everybody concerned. One volunteer had left permanently out of choice, another for a few days because of illness. Two couples were barely on speaking terms and the rest of the group were exhausted from the daily grind of cooking, collecting firewood and carrying water up from the tap by the river.

Life in the Iron Age was proving to be more of a challenge than anyone had ever expected.

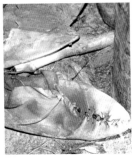

◁◁ The first shoes, despite being historically authentic, did not stand up well to everyday wear – especially walking on the gravel tracks.

◁ The replacement shoes were made of tougher leather and to a different design and they stood up better to regular wear.

▽ The state of your feet became a common topic of conversation during the project: Ron waxes lyrical to Emma (left) and Brenda about the state of his chilblains.

104

8

Performing

ONE WEEK INTO THE PROJECT AND THE ATMOSPHERE on the hillfort was very different. The volunteers had split into three sub-groups: the two older couples were in the chieftain's house, Bill and Yasmin had moved into the forge, which they found warmer, and the seven young people were still in their smaller house. But Nik's departure and the very public argument between the two sets of parents had unsettled the group. People were also finding the constant labour of carrying water and collecting firewood exhausting and, despite having modern non-slip soles glued to their Iron Age footwear, they still found the conditions slippery. The BBC had supplied all the volunteers with authentic leather shoes which were accurately modelled on a pair found in a grave in southern England. However, the soft leather deteriorated quickly in the muddy conditions and people's feet were constantly wet and uncomfortable. This only added to their general discomfort and air of lethargy.

Another problem the group faced was planning. They sometimes held several meetings a day to organize what needed to be done, but often the jobs were not followed through. Emma recalls, 'From my personal point of view, I was so sick of meeting after meeting after meeting. Then the Yasmin and Anne situation came up and everybody I think was really frustrated because we wanted to move on. But nobody knew how and that was really difficult … nobody could really see a way through and I think those pressures were bearing down on all of us.'

Although the volunteers were adamant that they wanted to stay on to the end, it was becoming clear that they and the BBC production team needed advice on how to break the state of lethargy and passivity which had descended on them. The BBC decided that the group would benefit from the motivational skills of a specialist and called in Phil Dale, a management consultant who had worked on previous BBC programmes. Not surprisingly, some of the volunteers were concerned about the effect an outsider might have on group dynamics, but Emma was relieved that a solution was being sought. 'I know that there have been lots of backroom chats about whether Phil should come. Obviously, suddenly bringing in someone from the outside is very difficult. It might make us feel like we'd failed in some way, whereas I was thinking, "Thank you God, you've sent somebody to kick asses."'

Phil arrived on the second Tuesday, ten days into the project, and immediately focused on what he saw as the main problem. 'There's a level of discord because the group is operating still as a group of individuals. So whilst individuals or small groups are being satisfied because they're doing interesting things, what is missing is a group collective to achieve a common goal. The biggest single issue, I think, is the fact that Anne has a very difficult role, in her eyes, to strike a balance between being a very forceful, controlling leader and just being somebody who is liked.'

It was a perceptive assessment and one that highlighted a fundamental difference between life today and how society would have been structured 2500 years ago. During the Iron Age, Castell Henllys would have been run by an autocrat – a warrior noble or chieftain who would have ruled the fort with an iron fist. Nobody would have dared to disobey an order. Without this dictatorial approach, a group of a hundred people or more on the hillfort would not have functioned efficiently or been able to organize themselves for the future. With inadequate preparation, this would simply have meant that they would not survive through the next winter.

However, this social situation is completely alien to people from the twenty-first century – only in the military would such a rigid command structure be tolerated today. However, the easy-going, consensual approach taken by the group was proving to be a luxury which the volunteers could not afford if they were to survive in the physically demanding and potentially hostile environment of the Iron Age. Perhaps with longer to adjust as a group they could have found a satisfactory way of working. But with only five weeks left to the end of the project, time was not on their side. Some of the volunteers, and Tom Little in particular, were also becoming weary of the bickering. 'It's been a weird time so far. There have been some arguments which were a bit stressful. I was hoping that everyone would get on straight away, but obviously certain things need to be sorted out and I should have realized that in the first place.'

Phil Dale spent a full day talking to each member of the group individually, including the BBC production team, to assess the group dynamics. In particular, he concentrated on Anne who had the difficult job of trying to be chieftain. 'What I've done with Anne is to give her feedback based on conversations with the whole group that says actually they're clamouring for somebody to give them some control. Anne felt that she was being too bossy – but when you talk to people, particularly Ron and Brenda and the younger people, they actually need to be directed. They need to have somebody who's on top of what they're doing.'

Phil Dale's intervention had a positive effect on morale. The group meetings became more focused, people were encouraged to talk with pride about their achievements and a proper agreement was reached about the priorities for the day, as Emma remembers. 'It felt like an inward spiral that was getting deeper and deeper into this terrible situation, and it was just really nice to have someone to come and look at the whole thing. It's like having a counsellor, really – it was like group therapy when Phil turned up.'

The BBC team were also involved in the self-analysis and they suggested changes to make life easier for the volunteers. The constant toil of bringing water and firewood up from the bottom of the hill was proving to be too great for people not used to heavy labour. If the volunteers were going to have the time and energy to carry out some of the 'time challenges' expected of them, then they needed to be relieved of some of these daily chores. During the Iron Age, much of this work would have been performed by a retinue of slaves and 'unfree workers', so it was agreed that unlimited firewood and charcoal should be brought up to the site. The water tap was also relocated at the top of the hill, inside the compound.

The BBC also gave the group two new 'time challenges', which were received enthusiastically. The first was an announcement that an 'Iron Age tribe', the Cantiaci re-enactment group from Kent, were going to visit for a weekend of feasting. The volunteers had eighteen days to plan for the visit, make gifts to exchange and prepare enough food for eleven visitors. The second challenge was for Samhain, their last night on the hillfort on 31 October. Samhain was the most important festival in the Celtic year and, as part of their celebrations, the volunteers were asked to build a wicker man, twenty feet tall. The prospect of two celebrations in quick succession delighted everybody, but there was much to do and plenty to organize.

On 28 September, the group also celebrated Ron and Brenda's thirty-seventh wedding anniversary. Chris, the tribal druid, presided over a moving ceremony in which the couple reaffirmed their wedding vows after more than a third of a century of marriage. Ron had often remarked that at fifty-nine, he was too old to be an Iron Age Celt: 'I'd have died off long before, mate!' In practice, their marriage had lasted longer than the lifetimes of most people living in the Iron Age. Brenda remembers the event with particular affection. 'It was a ceremony in which Chris, the druid,

△ Brenda and Ron, sporting their new iron necklaces.

took the service. It was in our roundhouse. He gave the blessing and then we reaffirmed our vows and we held hands. Chris wound a piece of material round both our hands and we had to bite on an apple and drink wine … then we did an odd sort of dance that Chris taught everybody. It was quite a funny dance, which made everybody laugh. They all enjoyed themselves and Ron and I were presented with a plaque that said *RB 37th* in clay.'

Once Phil Dale had left, everyone had more of a spring in their step. They were looking forward to the Cantiaci weekend and they were motivated to prepare for the visit. Chris, Bethan, Jody and Emma took it in turns to milk the goats in the morning and Chris started to experiment with making goats' cheese. The 'honey beer' was sampled, declared good and decanted.

MARRIAGE DURING THE IRON AGE

Women had power and influence during the Iron Age and there is evidence to suggest that the Celts thought of marriage as a partnership. Caesar wrote that once married, the men and women of Gaul would share their wealth. 'The men, after due reckoning, take from their own goods a sum of money equal to the dowry they had received from their wives and place it with the dowry. Of each sum account is kept between them and the profits saved; whichever of the two survives receives the portion of both together with the profits of the past years.' In this way, a woman who survived her noble husband could become wealthy in her own right.

Some Celtic chieftains and nobles might have practised polygamy and Caesar claimed that some women in Britain shared several husbands. Dynastic marriage was also common between the aristocracy of different tribes and clans. According to some classical writers, sexual relations amongst the Celts were more open than what they were accustomed to in Rome. The Roman senator Cassius Dio, for example, reported a harsh exchange between Argentocoxus, a female Celtic chieftain, and the empress Julia Augusta, when she was challenged about her morals. 'We fulfil the demands of nature in a much better way than do you Roman women: for we consort openly with the best men, whereas you let yourselves be debauched in secret by the vilest.'

▽ Emma and Bethan perfecting the art of making soft goats' cheese. They are filtering the whey through the cloth, leaving the semi-solid curd cheese.

TALLOW

You have been given a supply of animal fat from which you can make tallow.

Heat the fat slowly until it becomes liquid. Simmer for 30-60 minutes, then cool and strain through a cloth. Allow the fat to cool sufficiently so that you can safely add half of its volume in water.

Bring the fat and water mixture to the boil and simmer for 4 hours. Allow to cool again — you will be left with a thick disc of tallow at the top.

You can now make tallow candles, either by dipping wicks into the melted tallow or by pouring the tallow into a bowl containing a wick. You can make wicks from plaited wool or twine, dipped in beeswax.

To make soap, boil a thick mixture of wood-ash and water for 2 hours to make lye, then leave overnight to cool. Strain the lye through a cloth, but be careful, as it is caustic! Mix one pound of melted tallow with half a pint of lye. Boil, then simmer until milky.

To test, take a small amount and mix with hot water — the liquid should be clear and lather easily. If your test sample is satisfactory, allow the mixture to cool and then cut into blocks of soap.

Mark and Tom started talking about having a second attempt at making a charcoal clamp and several people started making pottery as gifts for the Cantiaci. Ron, Brenda and Bill began work on a furnace made from wattle and daub, which they would need to smelt iron, and they also began making a set of bellows. Young Christopher found plenty to do around the site, carving wood and gathering berries.

Bethan was also attending to her duties as teacher to Laszlo and Rosie and made clay letters and numbers as part of her teaching aids. The group were also given a new 'time challenge' to make tallow, which forms the basis of both candles and soap. Between them, David and Anne spent most of two days boiling down the sheep fat and following the recipe to the letter.

Only Yasmin found the week difficult. She was frustrated by having to keep a careful eye on two boisterous and inquisitive children. She could only find a couple of hours a day

△ Mark (sporting his new shoes) puts the final decorative touches to one of his pots before firing.

when Laszlo and Rosie were at lessons to get involved with the daily tasks. 'We don't want to be a burden and we don't want to have to go home – we won't go home, it's as simple as that. We want to make this work. But we need to be a community. We need to be closer and we need to be more communicative.' Relations with Anne were now more relaxed and for a few days at least, the group moved into a stage of 'performing'. Unfortunately, it was not to last very long.

For several days, four-year-old Rosie had been complaining of tummy pains. She was taken to the local surgery, where the doctor took a stool sample for examination and prescribed oral rehydration salts to give her liquid and sugar. But Rosie would not drink anything. Diluted Coca-cola, Lucozade, her favourite apple drink – everything was tried but Rosie wanted none of it. After three days of taking very little fluid and eating nothing, she was beginning to cause everyone concern.

Then on the Friday afternoon, less than two weeks into the project, a bombshell hit the group. A Food Safety officer from the local authority paid a visit with the news that Rosie's stool sample contained the bacteria campylobacter. This bacterial infection is becoming increasingly widespread and is now a common cause of gastroenteritis. It can be contracted from being in contact with contaminated water, unpasteurized milk or faeces and most commonly from eating raw or undercooked poultry. It causes painful stomach cramps and is contagious. It is also a reportable infection, which is why the Food Safety officer visited the site. The group were stunned. They had thought that their health problems of the previous week were behind them, but they were now faced with a potentially virulent bacterial infection. The morale amongst the group plummeted.

The Food Safety officer did not go up to the hillfort, but she did recommend that Rosie had a hot shower and a change of clothes. She also suggested ways in which the cycle of infection could be broken. All the utensils, cooking pots, cutting boards and buckets were taken off site for a hot wash in detergent. Washing powder and antiseptic disinfectant were brought up to the hillfort so that everybody could wash their clothing properly and all the volunteers were allowed a hot shower. Water from the mains tap, which had recently been relocated up on the fort, was sent away for analysis. Antibacterial handwash and scrubbing brushes for fingernails were provided to keep hands clean, disinfectant solution was brought so that the wooden utensils could be soaked overnight and everyone was given their own roll of toilet paper. When the buckets and cutting boards returned, they were carefully marked again for their different uses.

Perhaps most controversially of all, each of the volunteers was given a pair of wellington boots until more robust leather shoes could be made for them. Bill had cut his foot that weekend and although it was not serious in itself, everybody was concerned about the possibility of him getting a potentially serious wound infection. However, the wellington boots became symbolic of how much the twenty-first century had intervened in this experiment in living history. Everyone would have liked to have remained purist about the project, but nobody was prepared to turn away the offer of dry feet. The only person who objected to the changes was Chris Park, who seemed to have the constitution of an ox and was disdainful of introducing anything from the modern world. But even he eventually came to terms with the reality. 'Maybe I've got more of a tolerance of this kind of living, especially of the illness that has happened. I was upset to begin with, when I started to see these

▽ The volunteers carefully hid their wellington boots when the Cantiaci visited (see Chapter 10), but they magically re-appeared when they left and nobody was prepared to give them up.

things creeping in with all the twenty-first-century stuff … you're wandering about and you see a bright green thing hanging in the tree that you're supposed to squirt all over your hands, or you see a washing up bottle there, or a plastic bucket or bin liner full of charcoal. You know, it does make a general difference to the energy of the place. But that's okay, I'm not a purist, I'm into everyone having a nice time. If we hadn't made the changes, the project might not be still happening you know, so it was kind of a necessity really.'

The new health scare was a sudden reminder to everyone that we live in a world where we are accustomed to a clean and sterile environment and where we are protected from most infections and diseases. Chris Park experienced no health problems throughout his time on the hillfort, despite walking around most of the

MEDICINE IN THE IRON AGE

The Iron Age people were not totally lacking in medical knowledge and probably relied on a wide variety of herbal and natural remedies, many but not all of which have been lost through time. For example, the bark of the willow tree contains the same active ingredient as aspirin and can be an effective analgesic if a sufficient amount is chewed. (Our volunteers tried the remedy but found it tasted so horrible that they spat it out.) Violets too can have a mild sedative effect and the berries of deadly nightshade are a powerful heart stimulant (but not to be tried at home). Herbal poultices can be effective, and honey poured onto an open wound is a very good disinfectant. Urine, being sterile, can also be used to wash out a dirty wound.

The Iron Age Celts also believed in the power of their gods to heal, and this could well have had a potent effect. Even today, psychologists are still trying to understand the interaction between mind and body. It is reasonable to assume that a positive state of mind was just as effective in curing ills during the Iron Age as it is believed to be today.

Watery places had a special significance for the early Celts and they turned to them in times of need. Natural springs in Bath in England and in Nemausus (Nîmes) in France were used for their curative powers. At one site in the river Seine (whose name is derived from the Celtic goddess Sequanna), nearly 200 waterlogged wooden artefacts were discovered in 1963, including small wooden models of limbs, trunks and afflicted organs, and even complete statues. The figurines included representations of lungs and the respiratory system, breasts, eyes, a clubfoot and, most commonly, genitalia. The articles were carved from the heartwood of oak (itself a tree with spiritual significance for the Celts) and seem to have been created to appease the gods and to ask for favours. Even today, people are drawn to springs and pools and cast their own votive offerings into the water in the form of small coins, in the hope that their wish will come true.

The Iron Age people also attempted surgery. Several graves have been uncovered in central Europe containing specialized surgical instruments dating from around 300 BC, including retractors, probes and a trepanning saw. Trepanning is a surgical technique going back thousands of years, whereby holes are drilled in the skull to relieve neurological symptoms. A third-century BC skull recovered from Austria shows three trepanning holes drilled in the upper right forehead – the last of which is unfinished. The skull shows no sign of healing and the unfortunate patient probably died under the surgeon's knife – or, on this occasion, the surgeon's drill. Despite the serious nature of this procedure and the high chance of infection, other skeletal remains suggest that some patients did survive the operation.

Despite the obvious limitations in trying to assess the effectiveness of medical intervention for the Iron Age people, the combination of herbal remedies, faith, magic, and even occasional surgery was probably every bit as effective as the medicine practised by the Greeks and Romans at the time.

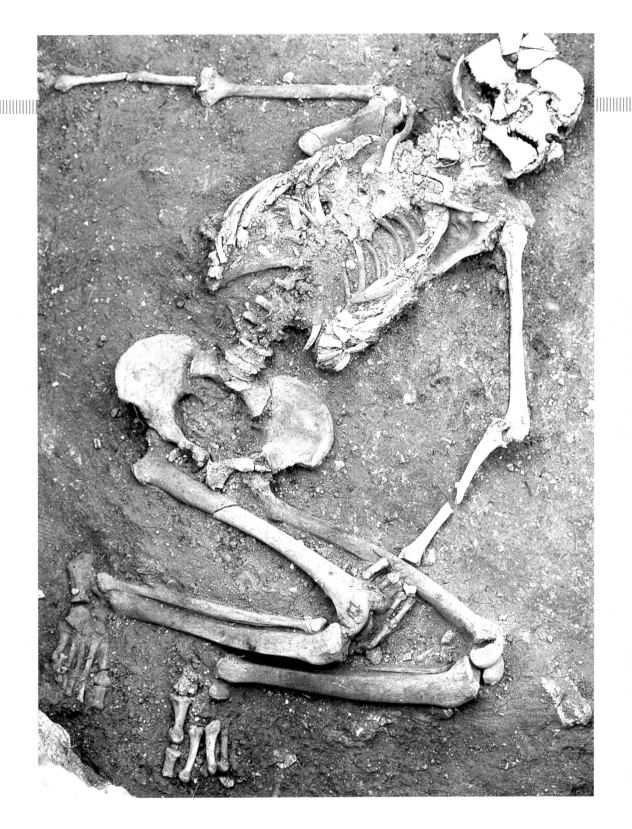

time in bare feet and not using the modern soaps. Possibly he had immunity against these infections, developed over months of living his 'alternative' lifestyle. Interestingly, the original Iron Age volunteers in the 1970s had very few problems with illness either, despite living in their settlement for a whole year. No doubt the Iron Age people too had a much more robust constitution than modern man, but the forensic analysis of skeletons found both in Britain and on the continent tells us that the Celts did suffer serious health problems.

Skeletal remains excavated at Danebury suggest that half of all children and a quarter of the adults had bone degeneration, thought to result from iron deficiency or anaemia. Poor hygiene, periodic malnutrition and medical ignorance resulted in poor health and disease amongst the Celts. Wounds become easily infected and septicaemia could be a swift killer until the early part of the twentieth century. For example, analysis of the skeleton of the Deal Warrior revealed a serious injury to his

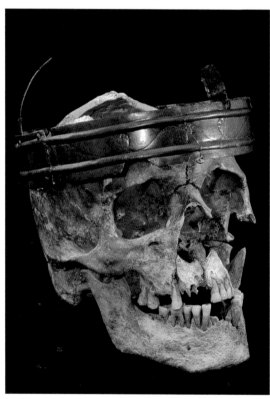

△ The skull of the Deal Warrior; the skeleton was found in a grave in Kent, having been buried in around 200–100 BC.

spine that had subsequently become infected. This left an abnormality in the healed area of his vertebrae, although the infection proved not to be fatal and he died of other causes.

Bone disease such as osteoarthritis of the spine and degenerative leg problems were common, especially amongst women, and this probably resulted from long hours spent squatting at menial tasks. At least a quarter of the adults showed signs of chronic back problems, suggesting that this debilitating condition is not restricted to modern man. Lindow man (the body of an Iron Age man found in a peat bog near Manchester; see page 134) was infested with roundworms, and intestinal worms and parasites were probably an endemic problem with the Celts.

If parallels with primitive societies today are appropriate, then children must inevitably have been most at risk. The Iron Age cemeteries in Yorkshire contain very few child graves, even though there must have been many child deaths. Perhaps children did not qualify for a formal burial, or perhaps they were buried elsewhere. However, in the very poorest parts of the world today, 30–40 per cent of infants die before they reach the age of five, and this percentage was probably true also for the Iron Age. At Danebury, it seems that a quarter of all children died before they reached their second birthday, but a surprising number also died between the ages of eight and twelve. Life expectancy *at birth* was therefore probably less than twenty years, but if you survived the hazardous years prior to adolescence, you could reasonably expect to live for another two or three decades.

Archaeologists can make an accurate estimate of age at death from excavated skeletons. The remains of adults in the Yorkshire cemeteries suggest that most adult males died between their late twenties and mid forties, women tended to die in their late teens or twenties and very few people lived beyond fifty. For men, there were the risks of meeting an untimely end through accident, war and personal conflict. In the Danebury burials, fifteen bodies showed weapon wounds and in thirteen cases death must have followed soon after injury, as healing had not begun.

The risks faced by adult men, however, were nothing compared to the hazards women had to endure during childbirth. Two women buried at Kirkburn in Yorkshire had apparently died during childbirth and were buried with their babies, but these were the only interred infants found in the cemetery. The constant risk from frequent pregnancy and childbirth probably explains the shorter life expectancy of women during the Iron Age, unlike today, when women on average live several years longer than men in all modern societies.

By the weekend, Rosie had made a full recovery from her illness. But on the Sunday morning, exactly two weeks into the project, Yasmin Billinghurst decided that she had to take her daughter home rather than run the risk of her contracting further infection. With the exception of the early tummy upset from the rich goats' milk, Rosie's brother Laszlo had been very fit and healthy throughout his time at the hillfort. But Yasmin, with great reluctance, decided that both children ought to leave.

Bill was now caught in a dilemma – whether he should go home with his family or stay with the group. In all the years they had been married, Bill and Yasmin had never spent a night apart. After much deliberation, Bill decided that he would stay to see the project through, providing he could have occasional phone calls home to his children.

▽ David and Bethan build a wattle and straw roof over the bloomery to keep the rain and wind away from the smelting process.

The following day, the Food Safety officer returned, but this time she asked to inspect the hillfort. Seeing that all her recommendations had been put in place, and more besides, she pronounced herself happy that everything possible had been done to prevent a recurrence of the health problem.

Now the volunteers had just two weeks to go before the Cantiaci arrived for the weekend, and it was decided that this would be a good time for Phil Dale to return to take a look at how the group was getting on. He was impressed with what he saw. 'There's a vast difference in many ways. I think the biggest thing is that the level of morale is massively higher than it was – now they're actually happier doing things. Last time I came they hadn't achieved very much at all other than survival, but if you go round today, the number of things that have actually been achieved by individuals is huge. They've put a roof over the furnace, they're starting to make jewellery, pottery, basketware. None of that was happening before, so it is a big change.'

There was now a very different atmosphere at the hillfort. The group were more purposeful, and more motivated; after two and a half weeks together, they were finally beginning to work effectively as a group. By the middle of the week, Ron and Brenda had finished the bellows and they could now start to operate the forge. Soon they had made their first piece of iron jewellery, and they had the rest of the group queuing up to learn the art of forging iron so that they could make their own. Ron and Brenda also finished the shaft furnace, but before they could attempt to smelt iron they had to fire it in order to vitrify the inside. This would require three separate firings, each hotter than the last, in order to make the inside lining hard enough to withstand the intense temperatures which would be reached when the smelting began.

The others also began to prepare for the Cantiaci visit. David tentatively began learning to weave baskets, Anne worked out how to use the loom and started to weave a rug, and Mark began making pots. Tom and Mark had a third attempt at making charcoal, but this time the charcoal burnt away.

During the middle of the week, western Wales was hit by the biggest storm of the year. The autumn had been unseasonably wet, but now the hillfort was blasted with torrential rain and winds gusting up to 70 mph. But inside the roundhouses the modern-day Celts were warm and dry, and their buildings stood up to the storm without any damage.

Unfortunately, things were not quite so easy back at home for Yasmin, as Bill realized. 'She's finding it difficult coping with Laszlo and Rosie, though she won't admit it. I think they're playing her up a bit and as her husband I think it's my role to be there to support her and also to help look after the kids. There's a lot for her to do on her own, especially with there only being a year between them, and they wind each other up and egg each other on. So I do feel quite sorry for her. I think she's got the rough end of the stick at the moment.' Bill was clearly beginning to have doubts about his decision to stay on the project.

A week after Yasmin and her children left the hillfort, she asked if they could return. All three of them were missing Bill, and Laszlo especially had not settled since they returned home. Rosie was back to her boisterous high spirits and both children were examined by their GP, who declared them to be fit and healthy.

This presented a dilemma for the volunteers as well as the BBC. The group had settled down during the previous week and were doing well at accomplishing their various Iron Age tasks. Although everyone enjoyed having the children around, the site was certainly a much more peaceful place without them. Emma, as always, was caught with one foot in the Iron Age and the other in the real world of the BBC. 'When we heard that Yasmin was thinking of coming back, I was quite surprised. I think everyone else was surprised too. And the general feeling was that Yasmin was well liked, the children were well liked, but I think there was some apprehension about how they would fit back in to the community. Anne had started to come out of herself and progress as a leader for us. And we were quite happy with the way things were going, even though we missed them as a family.'

The volunteers were not prepared to make a decision on whether Yasmin and the children should come back. In the end, the BBC decided that, in the overall interests of the project, it was probably better not to risk disrupting the group dynamics at this crucial stage. Yasmin was told that she could not return with the children. Not surprisingly, Bill was very disappointed at the decision and decided that his priority was to be with his wife and children. Reluctantly, he decided to leave the hillfort and return home.

The group was now down to just twelve individuals, but those who were left were beginning to grow together. Emma remembers this as a time when she really began to bond with the others in her roundhouse. 'The best times here are the evenings. You're inside from the rain and the cold and you have a really nice big fire. That's the time when we really get to know each other and we have been talking about quite personal things, and that's been really nice.'

▽ Bethan with the black sheep of the family – her favourite Soay which she named Suki.

PERFORMING

Bethan too began to sense a change in the group. 'I feel there is a real sense of community building now for the first time, you know. We're three and half weeks in and I think everyone's quite happy … people have had a good week and are genuinely happy here, and we're even saying that we don't want to leave.'

Halfway

THREE AND A HALF WEEKS INTO THE PROJECT, and life was beginning to look a little better for most of the volunteers …

Jody 'The weather's getting colder, but I'm so much happier. I'm really having a nice time now. I've got past that stage of worrying what people think all the time and I'm just getting on with it. So I generally feel much more at ease and much happier, and little things that were annoying me about people are easier to accept now. It seems not worth even worrying about, really.'

Mark 'We've passed the halfway stage now and everyone's enjoying themselves. I'm no longer wishing time away like I was in the first two weeks. We're starting to get more time to do our own projects. We're all wearing our little pendants, which is really nice. We all helped make our own – that brought everyone together in the forge and we all learnt a bit about blacksmithing. Ron and Brenda were really pleased that they could actually show off their skills.'

Chris P 'The leaves are turning on the trees, the acorns are dropping, the hazelnuts are falling and the seeds are heading towards the earth. So it's now October. I've had a kind of weird week. One day everything went wrong – I made a fertility rattle and put it in a tree and I reckon a fox or a magpie took it. I miss fruit – nice juicy apples – but I don't generally miss much from the twenty-first century.'

Bethan 'I cooked yesterday. I hate cooking. I really hate it. It's not a thing that I'm really brilliant at at the best of times with a cooker and a frying pan. I usually buy everything pre-packed. It's like – shove it in the oven and that's it! Cooking for seventeen people with nothing from the modern world is quite difficult. But Emma and I cooked some scrambled eggs and we were there all day! It was really warm in this Iron Age house, all smoky-eyed, but it was good fun. Nobody died and nobody complained about the food. It's going well.'

Ceris 'I've been talking to Bethan and I know I've got a big twang of Welsh. It's really annoying, but she says she's picking up my accent too! Yesterday I skinned two rabbits for dinner. I started making a big waterproof shawl-type thing with a hood. I'm just running a hot stone over the tallow now, to make it all melt. It feels good when you've actually got some projects on the go and you can really sit down and produce something.'

Tom 'During the last week things seem to have got quite a lot better. Nobody's been ill and everyone's getting on with things – apart from the last few days, which have been a bit frustrating for me because the charcoal didn't work at all. It all just burnt away. But today's been a lot better. I've made a little necklace thing, which we've all had to do, in the forge. We're also halfway through the whole project, which is good. The end is in sight – and everything's looking a bit better.'

Anne 'I really do miss my electric blanket. I miss electric light. I think it's very difficult to focus on the beauty of the place when you're living under such difficult conditions. I look around and I think, yeah, I just want to go home. I want to be warm. I want to be dry. It's difficult living in the community where everything is shared. You put something down and it disappears! I find it quite difficult sometimes just to be on my own or even to have a private conversation with Dave or Chris. Anyway, the sun is shining today – that's not a bad thing.'

David 'We've reached the halfway stage and I'd quite like to go home, really. I have never had great ambitions to live in a commune and I've proved that I don't make a very good commune person. We have very little time together as a family – partly because everybody else is all around in the community, but also because Anne is taken off as chief to liaise with the TV crew. But even at night, it is so cold that we have to sleep with all our clothes on, so there is no opportunity for intimacy of any kind, which is, I think, taking its toll. So that is one thing that we will probably make up for when we get back to civilization!'

◁◁ Dirty shoes off at the door!
◁ Chris samples the illicit brew of the twenty-first century.
▽ Blacksmiths' tools have changed little since the Iron Age –
much can be achieved with tongs, an anvil and a very hot fire.

9

The Tribe that Found a Name

THE MIDDLE OF OCTOBER BROUGHT MORE RAIN and gale-force winds and the worst floods for over fifty years began to wreak havoc throughout the country. After four weeks confined to the hillfort, the younger people in the group were beginning to get a little restless and wanted to know what was happening in the world outside. They had picked up some news from overhearing conversations between the film crew and visitors, and the occasional newspaper had mysteriously disappeared from the back of the producer's car. But the volunteers had been almost completely cut off from the modern world and they were keen for a bit of excitement.

It was Ceris Williams who provided the means for the great escape. Ceris had fully recovered from her attack of tonsillitis and had returned to the hillfort. Unknown to the production team, she had smuggled a £5 note and her debit card into the hillfort. 'We were a bit naughty because we did cheat a bit. I don't know if I can say much about that on camera because people who shouldn't find out will find out. But I'm sure it will all come clear.' This was their chance to break out of their Iron Age shackles. One night, when the older people in the top roundhouse had retired for the night, the seven younger people crept out of the compound and headed for the bright lights – or at least the neon lights of the nearest petrol station.

Bethan remembers the excursion. 'One night we were thinking, shall we just kind of see what's round the area? We'd heard from "a source" that there was a garage nearby, so we thought, right, we'll head for the garage … and lo and behold we got to the garage and it was shut! It was amazing – I could see all this food and drink inside.'

Everybody knew that leaving the hillfort meant they were strictly off-limits, but Emma tried to justify her own role in the affair. 'I didn't need to feel guilty because I took the video camera, which meant I was still working. I was doing my job, which was really brilliant, because I could be naughty and do my job at the same time!'

▷ Chris on the pole lathe. The rope is turned around the spindle, and is attached to a foot pedal at the bottom and to a flexible overhanging branch above. Pressing down on the pedal makes the rope turn the lathe.

With the garage closed and temptation only a pane of glass away, the group became more adventurous. Emma and the rest of them headed for the main road. 'All these people were passing in cars and I was sure they were freaked out of their minds seeing all these Iron Age people. We were trying to stop them to get directions to the nearest pub … We had this whole list of things that we thought we'd do to cheer ourselves up and one of them was go to the pub.'

It was another two miles along the road for the group to walk, dressed for the Iron Age but all wearing green wellington boots. 'We had a fiver between seven of us, but the barman was really sweet. I think he appreciated the predicament we were in. He helped us out with the drink and we're going to pay him back later.'

However, the break-out was not everything people had hoped for, as Emma admits. 'When we got in there everybody was quite subdued. Jody said that she felt very uncomfortable and I think a few people felt really guilty about it, that we'd let ourselves down.' Bethan, too, felt that way about the late-night excursion. 'I did feel really guilty actually. I did feel, you know, the BBC have given me this opportunity to live as an Iron Age person and I'm here in a pub! We all needed it and I think it was a good laugh, but we won't do it again.'

Not surprisingly, they were recognized in the pub and their secret was blown, but the excursion proved to be a big boost to morale and with only ten days to go before the Cantiaci re-enactment group were due to make their visit, the group were galvanized into activity. The forge was now fully operational and the area became a

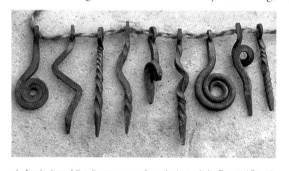

△ A selection of the diverse range of pendants made by Ron and Brenda in the forge using very basic equipment.

focus for the group. Ron and Brenda proposed that they should make pieces of iron jewellery as gifts for the visitors and produced a prototype. Soon a production line was in full operation to make enough for each of the Cantiaci.

The group had also been deliberating about their tribal name. They had agreed that they could not meet the Cantiaci without a clear identity and it was Ron's pendant which gave them an idea. The curved piece of iron looked like a snake and David suggested that they should call themselves the Serpentae, to remind them of the stream which snaked around their hillfort.

Meanwhile, Anne had begun to learn to use the weaving loom and was determined to complete a woven rug. She found the process very slow and time-

consuming, but she persevered to make a handmade woollen rug for the Cantiaci. Anne was also keen to experiment with primitive dyeing techniques. We know that three of the main colours of the Iron Age period were blue, yellow and red. They derived blue from woad (the leaves from a young plant give the best colour), weld offered various yellows, and red could be extracted from the root of the madder plant. Various plants gave other natural colours, including a rich purple from elderberry, a yellow-brown ochre colour from the flowers of St John's Wort, and golden orange from the chippings of yew wood. Colours could also be extracted from various lichens and tree bark.

Different procedures are used for different plants, but the colour is usually extracted by soaking the plants first in hot water. The wool is then soaked in the dye bath, and variations in colour can be obtained by mixing dyes or using additives. Some plant dyes impart their colour to the wool directly; others, called non-mordant dyes (from the French *mordre*, 'to bite'), require an additive to be effective. Early mordant additives included ash and stale urine, which are both sources of ammonia, and alum, a naturally occurring mineral salt.

Anne had been carefully collecting urine in a bucket to use as a mordant. The urine had to be stale, so it soon began to smell and was banished to sit under the eaves of the empty roundhouse and any passing males (film crew included) were invited to contribute. After two weeks, Anne considered the sample to be sufficiently stale and she used it to good effect to fix the woad-coloured wool.

▷ Anne especially worked hard to complete a woven woollen rug for the Cantiaci. She successfully obtained a blue colouring from woad – one of the traditional Iron Age colours.

WEAVING

The volunteers were provided with three warp-weighted looms at Castell Henllys, modelled on the type used during the Iron Age. The looms were positioned just inside the doorway of the roundhouse, where the weaver would benefit from the maximum light and could still work during bad weather.

Each loom was about 2 metres (6ft) high and was set permanently in the ground. The loom comprised a pair of wooden posts set vertically in the ground but leaning slightly backwards and joined top and bottom with horizontal beams to make a large wooden frame. Vertical woollen threads called the warp were suspended from the top bar and weighted at the bottom with triangular-shaped stone or pottery weights. These weights kept the warp under tension and are commonly found on archaeological sites.

About two-thirds of the way down the frame was a horizontal wooden rod, called a heddle bar, to which alternate warp threads were attached.

The heddle bar rested on wooden brackets fixed to each of the uprights. When the bar was drawn towards the weaver, it pulled open a gap between the alternating warp threads, called a 'shed'. The weaver was then able to pass a horizontal thread, called the 'weft', from one side of the loom to the other. When the heddle bar was released, the weights on the warp pulled the alternate threads backwards, thereby opening up a new shed. The weaver then passed the weft back in the opposite direction and the whole process was repeated.

To make a good quality, close-textured and hard-wearing cloth, the weft had to be kept tight and the weaver used a flat board called a weaving sword, which was inserted into the shed and used to hammer up the threads to keep the weft tightly woven. By the late Iron Age, most clothing was made from wool and some of the more sophisticated looms could produce more complex weaves such as herring-bone, a dog-tooth check and a broken diamond pattern.

The night before the Cantiaci arrived was the only full moon that the volunteers were to experience during their time at the hillfort. It was an opportunity for Chris to indulge in a spot of druidry. The popular image of modern druids is that of a group of men and women clad in white vestments, arms raised high, welcoming the sunrise at Stonehenge at the summer solstice. Like Chris Park, they are the modern practitioners of a pagan religion which has its roots in prehistory. We know a little about the original religion from the Roman and Greek writers and from early Irish texts, as well as from the archaeological record.

The druids were held in great reverence by the Iron Age people. When the Romans conquered the islands, they saw the power of the druids as both a social and a political threat, and from that point on, the religion began to decline and practically disappeared completely with the coming of Christianity. The modern religion of Druidism, typified by the ceremonies witnessed during the solstice at Stonehenge, dates from a renaissance of the religion in the eighteenth century. This, however, presents a problem in understanding the religion of the Iron Age people, for Druidism then and the practice of the religion today are not necessarily the same thing.

During the Iron Age, druids were more than just high priests – they held a unique social and political position in pre-Roman society. They presided over all public and private rituals involved with their religion, but they also acted in more secular matters as well. In a society with no tradition of democracy, human rights or written law, the druids probably acted as judge and jury, as Julius Caesar explained. 'In fact it is they who decide in almost all disputes, public and private; and if any crime has been committed, or murder done, or if there is any dispute about succession or boundaries, they also decide it.' However, these procedures only happened within the closed ranks of the elite and any form of independent arbitration was unlikely to be available to those of lesser birth.

The word druid is possibly derived from a mixture of languages: the first syllable most probably comes from the Greek word *drus*, meaning oak tree (which is sacred in Druidism), and the second from the Indo-European language root *wid*, 'to know'.

The name could also originate from the Gaelic word 'Druidh', meaning wise man or magician. According to the Roman historian Tacitus (AD 56–120), the main object of druidic worship was a great goddess, whose shrine was a grove of oaks growing on a British island.

According to Caesar, the position of priest, wise counsellor and judge required as much as half a lifetime of learning. 'Many young men assemble of their own motion to receive their training; many are sent by parents and relatives. Report says that in the schools of the druids they learn by heart a great number of verses, and therefore some persons remain twenty years

△ Druids in an urban setting on Primrose Hill with the London skyline in the background.

△ The summer solstice at Stonehenge has become a regular and popular gathering for modern druids, although their rituals probably have very little, if anything, to do with those of the early Celtic druids.

under training.' None of the information they received was ever committed to paper; instead they were said to learn large amounts by heart, which at least partly explains the long period of education.

Most of the volunteers at Castell Henllys quite happily tolerated the rituals led by Chris, but he was not a real druid and this was not something that he was used to doing. He was the first to admit that much of it was made up as he went along. 'Yeah, I mean I'm not really used to being a priest to a group of people, you know. That's not really my thing at all. I'm not here to say, "Right, I'm spiritual and I'm

THE END OF THE DRUIDS

Druids in continental Europe believed that their religion originated in Britain and their religious students travelled from Gaul to learn the druidic doctrines close to the heart of their religion – the island of Anglesey in north Wales. When the Romans conquered Britain in the first century AD, Anglesey inevitably became a target as the invaders sought to destroy the religion. The historian Tacitus wrote

△ The druids of Anglesey were massacred by the Romans by order of the governor Suetonius Paulinus.

about an attack on the island in AD 61 by the Roman governor of Britain: '… a garrison was set over the conquered islanders and the groves destroyed which had been devoted to their barbarous and superstitious rites; for it was part of their religion to honour their altars with the blood of their prisoners and to consult the gods by means of human entrails.'

Whatever the true nature of the religion during this period, the immense and unchallenged power wielded by the druids became a fundamental weakness of Iron Age society. The druids were secretive in the practice of their religion and drew their absolute authority from spiritual sanctions. The druid priests were not public leaders as we know them today, but 'controllers of a culture'; knowledge and learning were kept within an elitist cabal, and as a consequence their society was incapable of true social progress and development. The fanatical adherence of the Iron Age people to Druidism inevitably contributed to the destruction of their culture and to the downfall of their tribal nation.

gonna show you what that is, what that's not," so it's really different for me to have to be a kind of priest to a tribe. That's really weird. But other people have really come into their own sort of power as we've all shared parts during ceremonies, and they've really come alive as a group.'

These occasions were Chris's way of getting the volunteers to participate as a group. However, Bethan, who is a committed Christian, felt distinctly uncomfortable at times and usually stood outside the circle. 'I'll take part, but if there's anything that he's doing that I feel uncomfortable with, then I won't take part in it. Definitely not … my faith is with me here as well, you know. I'm a Christian here in this Iron Age twenty-first century.'

Ceris too found some of the rituals a little trying. 'The whole druid and witchcraft thing is something that I've been interested in. But I feel he imposes on us slightly. We're not allowed to eat until he's blessed the food or something. Well, I'm not bothered whether my food's blessed or not. I just want to eat it if I'm hungry. Basically, I think he talks a load of rubbish – but I probably shouldn't say that! When he's doing his ceremonies, he's laughing to himself anyway. He's laughing, so I don't know how seriously he actually takes it himself.'

Chris's celebration of the full moon was loosely based on modern druidism, but little is known of what really happened during the Iron Age ceremonies. Votive swords have been found with a moon carved on the iron blade and this suggests that the lunar cycle might have played a part in their rituals. Nevertheless, when it was totally dark, Chris took the group through an *ad hoc* ceremony. Four people stepped forward from the four points of the compass – east, south, west and north – to welcome the moon. It had been heavily overcast all evening, but at 8 p.m. a remarkable thing happened. The full moon, which was rising in the east, broke out of heavy cloud directly behind where Chris was standing, and for a brief five minutes the hillfort was bathed in the soft, blue light of moonshine.

Religion was almost certainly a very important part of life during the Iron Age but, in a society with no written texts and a druidic priesthood that was exceptionally secretive, there is little hard evidence on which to build a picture about this part of Celtic culture. As with everything else from the Iron Age, the usual sources need to be carefully considered before conclusions are drawn.

Archaeological evidence relies mainly on the excavation of graves and the discovery of votive offerings. There are many examples of Iron Age burials, often with accompanying 'grave goods', but nothing to match the large barrows and cairns of earlier times. It is possible that the Iron Age people might have practised cremation followed by the scattering of ashes and this would account for a lack of finds.

From the archaeological sites where votive offerings have been found, it seems that watery places – rivers, lakes and springs – were some of the most sacred sites to the Celts. Important artefacts have been found in the springs of the Roman Aquae

HUMAN SACRIFICE

The Celts were a superstitious people who lived in fear of their gods and there is abundant evidence to suggest that they sacrificed humans in an attempt to appease their deities. The classical texts hold many references to sacrificial rites. Caesar explained the importance of such events: '… those who are smitten with the more grievous maladies and who are engaged in the perils of battle either sacrifice human victims or vow to do so, employing the druids as ministers for such sacrifices. They believe, in effect, that unless for a man's life a life be paid, the majesty of the immortal gods may not be appeased.'

Strabo too explained how the Iron Age people believed they could foretell the future from the death throes of a dying victim. 'They used to strike a human being, whom they had devoted to death, in the back with a sword, and then divine from his death-struggle. But they would not sacrifice without the druids.'

Perhaps the most telling example of their faith in sacrifice is the death of 'Lindow Man'. In 1984, the well-preserved body of a man was discovered at Lindow Moss, an area to the south of Manchester used for peat extraction. The body was preserved because it had lain in waterlogged rotting vegetation which produced tannic acid, in conditions devoid of any oxygen. Radiocarbon dating found it to be nearly 2000 years old and it was sent to the British Museum for a detailed pathological examination. The corpse was that of a young man probably in

his mid-twenties, 1.69 metres (5 ft 6 in) tall, heavily built, in good health and with no congenital deformities. He had short straight hair (probably dark) and a neatly trimmed moustache and beard. His skin and fingernails were remarkably well-preserved. He was naked except for a fur band around his left arm. But it was the nature of his death that was particularly fascinating.

Pete Marsh, as he came to be known, was the victim of a ritual sacrifice. He had first been hit several times on the back of the head with an axe. He probably lost consciousness but he did not die instantly, as the wound on his head had swelled, which suggests that his heart continued beating for some time after the attack. A cord was then tied around his neck and tightened with such force that it broke his neck. His throat was then cut and he was thrown face down into a pool of water.

The remains of mistletoe pollen were found in his stomach. Mistletoe is often associated with druidic ceremonies, suggesting that this could have been a druidic sacrifice, or even that Lindow Man himself was a druid. Certainly he was a healthy young man and his fingernails were finely manicured, which suggests that he did not work as a labourer or slave.

Lindow Man is thought to have died a ritual 'three-fold execution' – he was hit over the head, garrotted and then drowned. Remarkably, his body showed no signs of restraint or struggle and it is

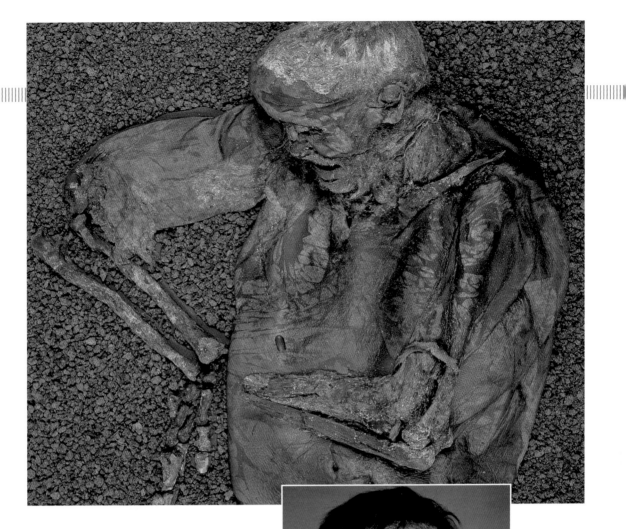

possible that he went willingly to his macabre death, perhaps as an offering or messenger to the gods, in the certainty that his place in the afterlife was assured.

Similar deaths are retold in the ancient texts, which include the story of a Scottish bard or druid called Lailoken, who allegedly fell from a cliff onto a spike projecting from a river. In this way he died from the fall, from impaling on the spike, and finally from drowning.

▷ An artist's impression of the likely appearance of Lindow Man.

▽ The bronze Battersea Shield has been dated between the third and first centuries BC and is a superb British example of later La Tène-style craftsmanship. The shield is over 60cm (2ft) long and was fabricated from over 90 separate components.

Sulis (today's Bath) and it seems likely that the curative power of the spring and its goddess Sulis was consciously sought. Archaeological excavations along springs feeding the river Seine in France have uncovered models of body parts, which also support the likelihood that the Celts considered spring water to have restorative powers (see Chapter 8, page 114).

Castell Henllys also had watery places which would have been important to its original inhabitants. At the bottom of the hillfort is a large expanse of swampy bog, which is exactly the type of place that held spiritual significance for the early Celts. The volunteers were also drawn to a spring at the side of the hill and this became a place for meditation and special gatherings of the group.

According to some of the epic poems, lakes were places where contact with the 'otherworld' was possible, so these must have had a spiritual significance. Many votive offerings have been found in lakes, confirming their status as sacred places. Rivers were also considered divine and several have been named after Celtic gods, including the Seine in France, the Boyne in Ireland and the Danube in Eastern Europe. The famous Battersea shield (left), recovered from the river Thames, is thought to be a votive offering. Woodland and trees were also places of devotion and these sites had associated gods and goddesses. The oak, the beech and the yew were all revered in Celtic Gaul, and the oak tree in particular is thought to have played an important role in druidic worship.

A number of isolated hoards found in the open countryside, such as the Snettisham hoard (mostly a collection of gold torcs, see page 8), could be interpreted as sacred offerings, suggesting that the earth might also have a religious significance. Skeletal remains (usually female) have been found buried below the gate area of some fortified sites and this suggests that human sacrifices were made to protect the gate. In some areas fences surrounded graves, which suggests that they were also considered to be revered places.

It is quite possible that the early Celtic people believed in immortality and that after death the individual would move on to the 'otherworld'. Strabo wrote, '… not only the druids, but others as well, say that men's souls, and also the universe, are indestructible, although both fire and water will at some time or other prevail over them.'

◁ Tom and Mark succeeded in firing a selection of pots as gifts for the visiting Cantiaci.
▽ The chief of the Cantiaci in fine fighting form.

10
Visitors from Another World

SATURDAY 14 OCTOBER MARKED THE END of four weeks at the hillfort. The volunteers were waiting for the visiting Cantiaci tribe with a mixture of excitement and nervousness. They were excited because these people were fanatical about the Iron Age and the volunteers knew that between them they had many different crafts and skills. After a month at Castell Henllys, they were keen to see any new faces. They were also nervous, because they were unsure how they would match up against enthusiasts who had immersed themselves in the period for years. However, as Ron reminded everybody, 'They might know a lot about the Iron Age, but we've been bloody well living it for the past month!'

The Cantiaci are one of several voluntary Iron Age 'living history' groups in Britain. They have their own Iron Age village in Gillingham in Kent and their aim is to show life as it might have been from around 80 BC to the Roman conquest in AD 43. (This was around the time that the occupation of Castell Henllys came to an end.) The Cantiaci have built their own Iron Age farmstead and they welcome school visits, free of charge, so that children can experience the sights, sounds and smells of the Iron Age.

The group had driven from Kent during the night and arrived in Wales at 6 a.m. After breakfast and a shower, they changed into their costumes and stepped into the Iron Age ready to meet the Serpentae. Relationships between tribes in Iron Age Britain were not always cordial and it was common for those who lived adjacent to each other often not to be friendly, whereas those who were more distant tended to have better relationships. In fact, tribal groupings throughout the Iron Age were often temporary as groups merged with others, perhaps through intermarriage, or were dominated by more powerful neighbours.

It was wet and rainy at midday when the Cantiaci arrived, in conditions reminiscent of the day of the volunteers' arrival. The Serpentae had worked hard rehearsing their welcoming ceremony and volunteers and camera crew alike understood exactly what was to happen. The plan was that Chris Park, the tribal druid, would welcome

The original Cantiaci

It is believed that the original Iron Age Cantiaci tribe were descended from Belgic and Gaulish migrants who crossed over to Britain from the Marne region of France, sometime between 200 and 150 BC. Probably trying to escape the Roman invasion of Gaul, they took refuge in Kent, where they established themselves somewhere in the vicinity of modern-day Canterbury.

The Cantiaci brought with them a different ceramic tradition and the remains of these pots suggest that the Belgic tribe did not move beyond the river Medway. When Caesar landed near Deal in August 55 BC, the Celtic tribes of Kent launched a surprise attack on the Roman forces with infantry, cavalry and charioteers. Their fighting zeal impressed Caesar, but the Romans were able to move inland and destroyed the hillfort at Bigbury before penetrating as far inland as Hertfordshire.

the Cantiaci at the gates of the hillfort, before taking them in for a formal exchange of gifts. However, on the day, at the first sound of the horn from the visiting tribe, all the planning was forgotten. Chris took off in full stride and met the Cantiaci half way down the hill – much to the confusion of the camera crew, who had to run after him to keep up. 'I went down to meet them and they were a really good bunch,' Chris said. 'They all had strange names and they were really full of spirit. And I brought them up to the little greeting ceremony and they had all these wonderful symbols and gifts with them … It was really nice to meet someone with that amount of knowledge and that empathy with what we were going through and how we were living.'

The Cantiaci were taken into the chief's roundhouse and welcomed yet again in another complicated ceremony conducted by Chris. Gifts were exchanged and the Serpentae went through an elaborate ritual dance, weaving their way between the visitors as they sang. Later in the afternoon, the rain eased off and the group moved outside, a little the worse for wear after sampling the honey beer.

The following day, Mark only had a vague recollection of what had happened. 'There were some bizarre events taking place yesterday and I got incredibly pissed, which was really good, except I couldn't remember a thing today. When I woke up, it took a bit of a while to come back to what I'd actually been doing. But everyone else took the piss out of me all day, which filled me in a bit on what I'd been doing. But I managed to get away without having a hangover. I had a pretty good time.'

Iron Age Britons loved a party too, but feasting in Iron Age Britain was more than an excuse to eat and drink to excess. The hierarchical structure of society and the importance of forging allegiances between clans and tribes meant that these occasions were important social and political events. Despite the riotous behaviour and heavy drinking that went on, these events were governed by all the formality and tradition which might be expected at the annual Lord Mayor's banquet. The Roman writer Athenaeus (quoting the widely travelled Greek philosopher Posidonius) reported, 'When a large number dine together they sit around in a circle with the most influential man in the centre like the leader of a chorus … Beside him sits the host and next, on either side, the others in order of distinction. Their shieldsmen stand behind them while their spearmen are seated in a circle on the opposite side and feast in common like their lords.'

Excessive indulgence was the order of the day and vast quantities of food and alcohol were consumed during the feast. Diodorus Siculus, also quoting Posidonius, wrote, '… beside them are hearths blazing with fire, with cauldrons and spits containing large pieces of meat. Brave warriors they honour with the finest pieces of meat.' The Roman writers describe the banquets in

△ The Cantiaci druid having one last puff from the twenty-first century, before visiting the Serpentae.

great detail; the participants gorged themselves on spit-roasted meat and bread, washed down with milk and beer. Bards sang eulogies to the partygoers accompanied by musicians playing the lyre, storytellers narrated genealogies and recounted tales of past heroes, and warriors took to boasting about earlier exploits.

It must have been good for male bonding, but inevitably things got out of hand. Rewarding favoured individuals with the finest cuts of meat led to petty jealousies and rivalry, which resulted in squabbles, drunken brawling and occasionally serious fighting, and more than one Iron Age noble met his maker over an argument about a leg of lamb. Athenaeus, again quoting Posidonius, described how the revelry could overstep the mark. 'The Celts sometimes engage in single combat at dinner. Assembling in arms they engage in a mock battle-drill, and mutual thrust-and-parry, but sometimes wounds are inflicted, and the irritation caused by this may lead even to the slaying of the opponent unless the bystanders hold them back.'

The revelry at Castell Henllys did not get *quite* as serious as it did during the Iron Age, but it is easy to understand how the festivities enjoyed by the Celts could get out of control.

THE CELTS AT WAR

Hostilities between warring tribes were traditionally short-lived affairs. Battles would rarely last more than a few days and would often be over before nightfall. The main objective was to establish the social ranking of either an individual or the tribe. The secondary objective was to define tribal boundaries and to provide an excuse to plunder. Tribal conflicts usually arose from raids between neighbouring tribes and these were often an opportunity for young warriors to prove themselves to their peer-group. Cattle (and occasionally women) were the main prizes; when raids got out of control, they could lead to more formalized conflict.

Full-scale battles were more of a theatrical performance than an act of war and rarely resulted in wholesale carnage. After the initial skirmishes and raids, the warring armies would confront each other, demands would be made and insults exchanged. The tribal elders, together with the women and children, would take a back seat and watch as their warriors rode their chariots up and down the enemy lines, casting abuse at their opponents. A cacophony of horns and beating of shields accompanied this display of belligerent one-upmanship. Usually, the armies would select a warrior for one-to-one combat with the enemy, and when this contest was resolved, both sides would accept the result and retire. But when real conflicts occurred, they were grim events and gruesome injuries are found in the archaeological record.

One of the features of Iron Age battle was the two-horse chariot, which combined the desire for flamboyant showmanship on the battlefield with an effective fighting weapon. At its best, the chariot was a sophisticated piece of machinery, with circular iron hoops which acted as protective tyres on the wheels, and iron caps on the axles to protect the hubs and to retain the axle pins which kept the wheels in place.

The ordinary foot soldier had to make do with rather more prosaic weaponry. The great stand-by were sling stones – round, water-worn pebbles which were collected ready for use and stored by the thousand in hillforts. A continuous volley from a company of experienced slingers could have a devastating effect on an opposing army.

The Iron Age warrior also used iron spears, javelins, swords and daggers. The swords often had elaborate decoration around the hilts and many of the weapons were quite sophisticated; the shape and design of the blades were intended for very specific uses, such as throwing, thrusting or tearing. Diodorus Siculus observed, 'Some of the javelins are forged with a straight head, while some are curved with breaks throughout their whole length so that a blow not only cuts but also tears the flesh and the recovery of the spear rips the wound open.' The quality of iron used to make these weapons varied and Roman writers commented on warriors having to retire from the battlefield to straighten their swords.

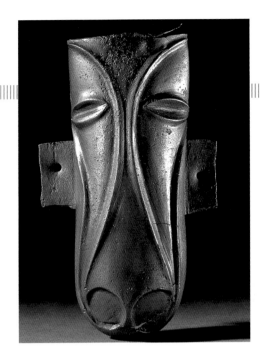

Some Celtic warriors went into battle naked, while others were better protected with a helmet and shield or even an iron breastplate of chain mail. Occasionally, even their horses were adorned with masks and pony-caps (*chamfreins*), creating an impressive spectacle on the battle-field. Trumpets were also used, no doubt to rally warriors, to frighten the enemy and probably also to convey signals to the warriors.

Diodorus Siculus reported on the custom of removing the heads of slain warriors on the battle field. 'When their enemies fall they cut off their heads and fasten them about the necks of their horses; and turning over to their attendants the arms of their opponents, all covered in blood, they carry them off as booty …' The classical writers were appalled at this desecration, but the heads could have been battle trophies, proof of a warrior's courage – or the practice may even have had religious significance.

The following morning, the Cantiaci and the Serpentae spent time together, sharing ideas and advice. The Cantiaci blacksmith joined Ron and Brenda in the forge, and the couple looked enviously at his set of tools which he had modelled on those found at Danebury. Remarkably, they were very similar to what a blacksmith would use today. The Cantiaci potter showed Mark and Tom how to make coil pots and the women shared ideas on dyeing and weaving. The Cantiaci had also brought a whole salmon as a gift and Anne was shown a novel way to cook it over an open fire. 'She put it in some soft pastry dough – just flour and water – and just threw it on the fire. The dough baked really hard, for two hours maybe, and it ended up look-ing like a log. In fact Dave nearly threw it on the fire as a log and we had to remind him it was in fact a piece of fish. But it tasted absolutely fantastic. She wrapped it in leaves first and then put the pastry case around it and it kept it so moist and so tasty that I'm definitely going to try that when I get home.'

At midday, the two tribes gathered at the sacred spring and Chris went through another elaborate ceremony, this time for departure. Then Ron and Brenda gave each of the visitors a hand-forged iron serpent as a memento of the time the two tribes came together.

143

▽ A statue of Boudica and her daughters, erected in 1902 at the northern end of Westminster Bridge in London. The blades on the wheels are a romantic invention.

The Roman invasion

Prior to the Roman invasion, the British tribes were essentially volatile and unstable, but the presence of foreigners in the country galvanized some of them into collaborative defence. The formalized and protracted battles against the Romans were very different from the conflicts the Iron Age warrior was used to fighting. Although the British tribes eventually capitulated to the Romans, they did have notable early successes against the better organization and greater discipline of the Romans, as Julius Caesar found to his cost in 55 and 54 BC. Even when the Romans returned in AD 43, they were met with patchy but sustained insurgency.

By AD 50, most of the tribes in southern and central England were under the control of the Roman Army. Wales proved to be more difficult to contain and the Romans spent several years fighting the Welsh tribes before pulling back to handle the revolt of the Iceni led by Queen Boudica in AD 60 or 61. She was perhaps the most famous of several military leaders who organized resistance to the invaders. The Roman senator Cassius Dio wrote, 'It was especially shameful for the Romans that it was a woman who brought all this upon them … this was the work of Buduica (*sic*), a woman of the British royal family who had uncommon intelligence for a woman.'

The warrior queen plundered the Roman garrison in London and Dio reported unspeakable reprisals on the inhabitants. 'Every kind of atrocity was inflicted upon their captives, and the most fearful bestiality was when they hung up naked the noblest and best-looking women. They cut off their breasts and stitched them to their mouths, so that the women seemed to be eating them, and after this they impaled them on sharp stakes run right up the body.'

Boudica then raised an army of about 120,000 warriors to face the Romans. As she prepared again for war, Tacitus records that she rode up in her chariot and addressed each tribe lined up for battle. 'We British,' she cried, 'are used to women commanders in war. But it is not as the descendant of mighty ancestors that I fight now, avenging lost kingdom and wealth; rather as one of the people, avenging lost liberty, scourging the violation of my daughters. The lusts of the Romans are gross; they cannot keep their filthy hands from our bodies, not even from the old or chaste … you must either win on this battlefield or die. That is my resolve, and I am a woman; men may live and be slaves.'

On this occasion, Boudica lost the battle and the war. After the suppression of the Iceni, the Romans worked their way north and west through the country, suppressing the Welsh tribes and then, by AD 84, the Caledonian tribes in Scotland. However, the Romans did not have sufficient troops to contain Scotland and, by the middle of the second century AD, Hadrian's wall became the northern limit of their empire.

With the visit of the Cantiaci behind them, the volunteers settled down to the last couple of weeks in the Iron Age. They still had much to accomplish: Ron still had not tried to smelt iron, Mark and Tom had unfired pots, Ceris wanted to carve a figurine to cast in bronze, and they all had to start work on the wicker man. But the priority for the moment was Jody's twenty-first birthday on Tuesday 17 October. Ron made her an iron wristband as a present from the group, and Emma and Mark planned another late-night sortie into the modern world. On the Monday night they broke the rules a second time and went shopping for birthday food. As Mark remembers, the plan backfired. 'We bought so much food that people were feeling sick just trying to cram in the last bit of chocolate. I think we went a bit overboard and I think other people felt guilty about it as well.' Their overindulgence was not helped by the production team, who also broke the rules and made Jody a birthday cake – covered in chocolate!

Jody had no regrets about spending her special day in the Iron Age and declared that she would not have wanted to be anywhere else. 'It was an amazing place to be on my twenty-first – just lying there last night listening to everyone chatting. Everyone was saying

△ Jody's 21st birthday cake – the volunteers experienced a sugar and chocolate 'high' which lasted several days.

to me, "Don't you wish you could be at home having a party?" But this is way more special and exciting and I'll never forget it. We had some honey beer so everyone was merry, we were sitting around the fire singing songs and everyone was being really humorous and amusing me. I was the queen, so I was allowed to say what I wanted, and everyone was looking after me and getting me cups of beer.'

The Celts too marked major events in people's lives, although becoming 21 was probably not one of them! According to Irish texts, they held a name-giving ceremony when a child was accepted into the community. The texts also hint at rituals for young males when they were initiated as warriors and rituals before marriage. Kings also underwent elaborate crowning ceremonies.

Meanwhile, with Jody's birthday over, the volunteers got back to their 'time challenges'. Mark and Tom had made several ceramic pots which had been gently drying out ready for firing. In fact, there was very little pottery at Castell Henllys during the Iron Age period and the original inhabitants probably used wooden plates and bowls instead. This was a common situation in northern and western Britain, probably due to the poorer quality raw materials which produced less resilient pots. However, elsewhere in southern Britain it was an important industry and ceramic pottery was widely used for storage, preparation, cooking and transportation.

The raw materials for ceramic pottery were easily obtained. Clay was mixed with 'temper' such as crushed flint or sand, which reduced shrinkage and cracking. The Iron Age potters were skilled at controlling the colour of the finished article. By varying the amount of oxygen in the firing, they could change the colour of the finished pot from black through to grey or red. On the continent, high-quality vessels were produced on a potter's wheel from as early as the fifth century BC. However, this technique was not introduced into Britain until the end of the Iron Age, so British pots were hand-made by coil- or slab-shaping. Without a wheel, the finished article is coarser.

POTTERY

You are short of bowls and pots, so this is a good time to make your own.

To fire your pots, first try a pit clamp. Line the base of a pit with hot embers, followed by two or three layers of green wood, then place your pots on top. Next, pile dry wood on the pots to make a mound, followed by damp straw. Finally, cover with soil.

Leave for 24 hours, but keep the covering of soil intact. The reducing atmosphere in the clamp should produce blackened pottery – the most common type of Iron Age pottery.

For your second batch, you must use the up-draught kiln. This can achieve temperatures of well over 900°C and will turn clay into red oxidized earthenware. Gently warm the kiln first, then select a small member of your tribe to place the pots on the earth shelves inside the kiln.

For the best results, slowly raise the temperatures of the kiln by about 100°C an hour, although you will have no way of recording the temperature. The process will take a full day.

Mark and Tom first tried to fire their pots using a pit clamp, which was similar in principle to the charcoal clamp. They lined the base of a pit with hot embers, followed by two or three layers of green wood, then they placed their pots on top. Next, they piled dry wood over the pots to make a mound, which was then covered with damp bracken and soil. They then left the clamp to burn out over a couple of days. This technique is notorious for its low success rate, but Mark and Tom were delighted to find that about 20 per cent of their pots were intact – about average for a pottery clamp.

For their second batch, they used an up-draught kiln which had been built on the site during the summer, ready for use during their stay at the hillfort. The up-draught kiln is made from a framework of hazel branches covered with daub and is a much more sophisticated way of firing pottery that was used during the late Iron Age. It can achieve temperatures of over 900°C, but it requires careful firing. The pots are placed at the far end of the kiln on earthen shelves situated below the chimney. Then a fire is lit at the mouth of the kiln and gently brought up to temperature. In order to stop the pots from cracking, the temperature has to be raised very slowly, although of course they had no method of recording it. The process took Tom and Mark long into the evening and then they had to leave the kiln for a further two days to cool down. However, their patience was rewarded with an almost 100 per cent success rate. Mark found the process very rewarding. 'To start from the beginning, to make your pots from clay and then fire them in the way the Iron Age people did, was really satisfying. But it did take a really long time, because you had to leave the pots for two weeks to dry out before putting them in the kiln.'

Meanwhile, other members of the group were out on a field below the hillfort, trying to come to terms with ploughing Iron Age-style. The coulter plough, which turns the topsoil, was not developed until the Roman period. Instead, the Celts used a more primitive device called an ard. Because the ard only breaks up the soil and does not turn it over like a plough, Iron Age fields were often ploughed twice in opposite directions. Chris found this a very effective technique. 'The first time we ploughed, the field was really difficult – the soil was packed hard. But then we ploughed it a second time at right angles and it really worked well. Now we've planted winter wheat and I want to come back in the spring to see how it's grown!' The criss-cross pattern made by double ploughing with an ard during the Iron Age can still occasionally be identified in aerial photographs.

▽ The stoker's-eye view of the up-draught kiln. Tom and Mark had to be careful to raise the temperature slowly in the kiln to prevent the pots cracking from uneven heating.

▽ Emma at the helm with Chris and Mark pulling the ard. It was necessary to plough the field in opposite directions to break the soil – just as they did during the Iron Age.

The Celts would probably have used cattle to pull the ard, but it takes several months to train a team to pull a plough, so the volunteers had no choice but to haul the ard themselves. A typical Iron Age field varies between one tenth and one quarter of a hectare (one fifth and one half of an acre), representing an area which could be worked in a day. Even today, the pattern of Iron Age field systems can still be identified in the British countryside. The outline of the boundaries is best preserved where there has been little agricultural activity during the last two thousand years, such as on hillsides which are too steep for modern agriculture. These fields can usually be identified by 'lynchets' or low banks, which outline their shape. Lynchets are formed by the natural movement of soil down a slope during ploughing, and a hedge or fence often acted as a barrier to the flow of soil.

Iron Age crops

Seeds and plants do not normally survive over thousands of years unless they are subjected to special conditions which help their preservation. For example, seeds can become carbonized in a fire, which stops them from deteriorating. Other plants might become preserved in peat bogs or in other conditions where oxygen is excluded (anaerobic conditions). It is from these sources that archaeologists are able to identify the types of seed grain used by the early Celts.

During the Iron Age, the most commonly cultivated crops included emmer wheat, spelt wheat and hulled six-row barley, all winter-sown varieties. Winter sowing had a big advantage for the Iron Age people because it spread the labour of harvesting across the year and a crop which ripened early the following year offered a supply of fresh food when supplies stored over the winter might be running low.

Agricultural techniques were simple and labour-intensive. The crops were harvested using a small iron sickle, before being cleaned, threshed and winnowed. The grain would then be divided into three groups – for human consumption, seed and animal feed – before being stored. The grain for consumption would be ground by hand on quern-stones to make flour for bread. Alternatively, it could be added to soup to make a gruel. Barley could also be used to brew beer. It has been estimated that 1 cubic metre (35 cubic ft) of grain would provide enough food for two people for a year.

Emmer and spelt wheat have a particularly high protein content – 20 and 19 per cent respectively (dry weight) – compared to just 8–9 per cent protein found in modern varieties. This would have been a big advantage for Iron Age people, who survived on a very limited diet by modern standards.

As the group moved into their final two weeks, the weather improved (at least briefly), the sun shone and their spirits soared. The Cantiaci visit had been a success and gave them new-found confidence, and as a group they were more settled and more comfortable than ever before. Anne in particular was feeling much more relaxed. 'We really are having quite a good time now. It's still quite uncomfortable in bed and things like that, but we can cope with that now. We've sorted out blankets and shawls and things, so we're quite cosy at night, we don't have to worry too much about that, even though the nights are getting a bit colder.

I think we really have gelled into a group. It's almost like a small family now and everyone's getting on so well. Everyone's having a laugh and singing together and it makes such a big difference.'

Anne's twelve-year-old son Christopher was happy too, having fulfilled his ambition to live in the Iron Age. 'I'm having a great time at the moment. We're into our fifth week now and we've got to do so many challenges. We've planted a field –

STORAGE PITS

It was essential for the Iron Age people to store their grain throughout the winter, or for times of shortage. Castell Henllys, like many hillforts, was probably used as a community storage centre (see Chapter 5, page 61), and surplus grain was stored in four-post granaries with a raised floor, to allow air to circulate. However, in many hillforts in southern Britain, and especially in chalk, gravel or sandy areas, surplus grain was stored underground in storage pits – essentially a prehistoric underground silo. These storage pits are probably the single most important piece of common evidence available to archaeologists studying the Iron Age.

Storage pits come in many different shapes and sizes, from a few centimetres to over 3 metres deep (over 10ft). Sometimes they were cylindrical, but more often they tapered from bottom to top, called a 'beehive' pit. They were used for many different purposes and sometimes a pit might have been used for different things at different times, making interpretation of the archaeology difficult. Even so, pits are very useful because their careful excavation can give important clues to how the Iron Age people lived, ate and even worshipped.

Normally grain must be dried before storing, but in a storage pit the recently harvested grain was poured straight into the excavated pit and then sealed with an airtight plug of clay. As soon as the pit was sealed, the grain in contact with the air trapped under the clay plug began to germinate, which produced carbon dioxide. This gas is heavier than air, so it sank through the stored grain, inhibiting any further deterioration for several months or even years. It was an ingenious solution to long-term storage and less than two per cent of the crop was lost through deterioration.

However, what makes the pits particularly interesting is what happened to them once they were no longer used for grain storage. Old storage pits are often found filled with rubbish, which is a treasure trove to any archaeologist. On other occasions, they are found filled with offerings to the deities, including animal and human bones and sometimes complete skeletons. This suggests that placing the grain close to the 'underworld' held a deep religious significance for the Iron Age Celts, who used the pits to make offerings to their gods in gratitude for the grain's safekeeping.

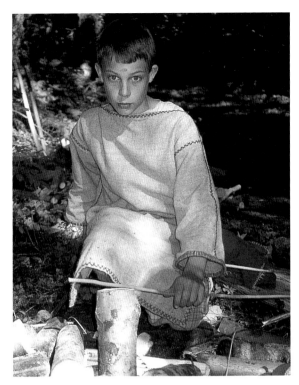

△ Big Chris would quite happily have stayed on at Castell Henllys indefinitely.

◁ Living in the Iron Age was a dream come true for little Chris. 'I feel more grown up than when I first came. I think one of the reasons is because I've probably been doing a lot more grown-uppy-type things.'

that wasn't too major – but we've got to make a wicker man. We've got to smelt some iron – that's Ron and Brenda's thing. So I'm having a great time … I'm really enjoying myself.'

With only a fortnight to go to Samhain, some of the volunteers were even beginning to have doubts about wanting to leave. Jody Elphick in particular had settled into a comfortable routine. She had been fit and well throughout her stay on the hillfort and was beginning to talk about how much she would like to stay on. 'I just don't feel like six or seven weeks is going to be enough at all. I've started thinking about what it's going to be like going back to our normal lives and I don't know if I really want to. Which is bizarre, because I never would have thought I'd say this at all, but I really feel like this is my home now. Just living outdoors and not having to worry about stupid things like brushing your hair, putting on your make-up, going out to work. It's a completely different existence here.'

Not surprisingly, Chris Park was also in his element and he would happily have opted to stay too. 'I really don't want to leave. I could move into the middle round-house and just live there. I could easily do that. Not on my own of course, I'd need people and animals and the BBC to bring me food. We've had it really easy, actually. We haven't had to get in a harvest, we haven't had to work our arses off. Physically, we haven't had it hard.'

153

◁◁ Dave works on the head of the wicker man.
◁ Ceris carving a wax boar as a mould to cast in bronze using the *cire perdue* (lost wax) technique.
▽ The eve of Samhain and their last night on the hillfort – the new Iron-Agers celebrate the end of their stay at Castell Henllys in true Celtic style.

11

The Iron Wizard

THE LAST FULL WEEK BEGAN BADLY FOR EVERYONE, with the worst storm of the year. Around 80mm (over 3in) of rain fell in one day, which led to widespread flooding throughout the country, and severe gale force winds blasted the west coast of Wales with gusts of up to 90mph. The combination of flooding, fallen trees on the railway lines and a nationwide inspection of track in the aftermath of the fatal Hatfield crash led to widespread cancellation of trains throughout the country – with no trains at all running in Wales and the West Country. In these circumstances, who would want to go back to the twenty-first century?

However, autumn was also bringing cold winds and most people were feeling the chill. The women decided that authentic or not, they would do something about their lack of underwear, and they set about making 'Celtic bloomers'. For Brenda, they were a big improvement in her life. 'It's been freezing cold most nights, the beds are uncomfortable, if you have to get up at night there's no light and the toilets are about a quarter of a mile away. I haven't cleaned my teeth properly since I came and I haven't washed my hair for days. But at least I've got myself some knickers at long last!' Mark too was suffering in the cold weather and noticed a change in people's attitudes. 'I think everyone is really feeling the cold and starting to get a bit down – there's definitely a noticeable change in the atmosphere in the camp at the moment. Recently I've noticed that everyone is getting up really late and just lazing around. I think it's something to do with the fact that there's only a week left.'

The volunteers were also finding that the limited Iron Age diet was becoming tedious. The days of hazelnuts and berries were now long gone; lamb and kale every night was beginning to lose its appeal. Tom, who'd been apprehensive about Iron Age food from the start, found that it was really beginning to get to him. 'I just want to eat some nice food. Just eating lamb and kale and peas is starting to piss me off now. I really need some good food and something nice to drink apart from bloody water and goat's milk. Ugh!'

Even mild-mannered Bethan was beginning to feel strongly about the food. 'I'm truly pissed off with lamb! I've eaten so much lamb over the past two weeks that I don't want to see the stuff again. Also, this kale that we've been eating – I never thought you could cook kale in so many different ways!'

Yet despite the weather and the monotonous diet, the volunteers still had to prepare for their final night in the hillfort. Dave Rickard had begun to learn the rudiments of basketmaking and set about making the head for the wicker man. Further down the hill, Chris was organizing the construction of the main body, close to the site where it would be erected and burnt. 'The wicker man is coming along really well. We stood him up on one leg the other day and he's quite strong. The Celts really revered the head as being the seat of the soul and when we attach the head to the body, it's going to look so spooky.' Ceris was proving to be a talented sculptress and had turned her attention to carving a small boar from beeswax, with the intention of using it to cast a bronze figurine.

△ Ceris's wax boar figurine. Unfortunately Ron could not get the bronze sufficiently hot to pour into a 'lost wax' mould.

The greatest pressure, however, was on Ron and Brenda. They had been asked to make a variety of Iron Age objects in the forge, but they were falling behind schedule. Ron had to forge a sword for Samhain from the iron currency bars supplied by the BBC, beat out a drinking chalice from a disc of bronze, make a mould of Ceris's wax boar to cast the bronze figurine, fire the shaft furnace and try to smelt iron. This last task was, without doubt, the most difficult Iron Age challenge of all.

The votive sword was a straightforward task for an experienced blacksmith. The only problem was that the charcoal fire in the forge could not accommodate a long length of iron. However, Ron was able to build a makeshift forge in one of the other roundhouses that would accommodate it. The Iron Age blacksmith would have worked his bar of iron in exactly the same way as Ron, alternately heating the metal white-hot and then hammering it into shape before it cooled and was no longer malleable.

△ Ron displays his drinking crucible formed from a simple disc of bronze, in preparation for the Samain celebrations.

Ron also 'tempered' the sword using the old iron-making technique, described in Chapter 4, of reheating quenched iron to a moderate temperature and then allowing it to cool slowly to make the metal much less brittle. This process could be used to make iron weapons and tools that combined the best of hardness, strength and flexibility.

As Ron continued to re-heat the iron sword over a charcoal fire, another important process was beginning to occur. The surface layer of the white-hot iron was beginning to absorb carbon from the charcoal to produce a primitive form of steel. This, combined with tempering, would produce a hard, strong sword which would be much sharper than a simple iron weapon. In this way, Iron Age black-smiths could produce high quality iron weapons and tools for their people. It is little wonder that smiths were held in such high regard by the early Celts and began to take on the role of folklore magicians and wizards. Their secret was that they had discovered the method, if not the science, of making steel.

The final Iron Age challenge left for Ron and Brenda was to smelt iron from ore. The Iron Age blacksmiths produced tonnes of iron using charcoal-fired shaft furnaces, but it is a technique which defeats most people who try it today. Ron had been a blacksmith all his working life and to succeed in smelting iron using Iron Age techniques was the main reason why he and Brenda had joined the project.

Smelting iron is a much more complex process than working copper or bronze and it uses much more fuel. Iron remains solid at temperatures below approximately 1500°C (2700°F). However, the furnaces used during the Iron Age could only achieve temperatures in the region of 1200 to 1400°C (2200 to 2550°F), so the early smiths were never able to actually *melt* iron.

Ron's one ambition in the Iron Age was to succeed in reaching the smelting stage and to make an iron bloom. 'Our chances were slim because so many people had tried this and failed. I was worried about weighing out the ore and the charcoal to get the right mix. We had to cheat and I used a one-litre water bottle which we knew weighed one kilo when it was full. Once I was sure I'd got the weights right, I thought our chances were 50–50.'

Ron and Brenda used a crude shaft furnace, based on the design archaeologists believe was used during the Iron Age. It was made from wattle and daub, approximately one metre (3ft) high. At the lowest point of the furnace was a large hole called a tapping arch, through which the slag runs out. On the opposite side was a 'tuyere' hole, through which a set of bellows can force air. During the previous few days, Ron had prepared the furnace by firing it first with wood and then with charcoal, progressively increasing the temperature until the inside of the furnace was vitrified and ready for the intense temperatures required to smelt iron.

On the first day of smelting, Ron started the fire at 9.40 a.m. to warm up the furnace. By 11.45 a.m. he had blocked off the tapping arch at the base of the furnace with turf to retain the heat, and Chris Park began pumping the bellows. By 1 p.m., Ron was ready to put in the first charge of charcoal and ore. He used a soft red ochre iron ore, which is the easiest ore to smelt, in a ratio of one part ore to two parts charcoal. The best charcoal to use is alder, which burns hotter than any other. However, by 1.30 p.m., they discovered a design fault in the bellows. During the in-draught stage of the action, the bellows sucked a back draught of hot air in from the furnace and the intense heat burnt out the leather valve inside the bellows. Ron went back to the drawing board.

The following morning, Ron and Brenda were back with the rebuilt bellows. However, before they even got to the stage of adding the iron ore, the bellows started to overheat again. 'That second attempt was even worse because I could see things were going wrong right from the start!' By 1.30 p.m. the bellows had caught fire again and Ron was on the point of abandoning the 'campaign' for a second time when a modern set of bellows was found at short notice. Without them, the smelt could not have continued.

Throughout the afternoon, Ron added more charges of ore and charcoal mix to the furnace and in order to maintain the temperature, the bellows had to be worked constantly. Everyone got involved – the volunteers, the BBC team and the staff at Castell Henllys all took turns to pump air into the furnace. Ron was able to estimate the temperature inside by peering through the tuyere hole and checking the colour of the flame. By mid-afternoon, he estimated it had got up to an encouraging 1300°C. At this temperature a process called sintering begins to take place, as fine particles of iron begin to congeal. Any silica present in the ore forms a slag, which flows out through the tapping arch in the bottom of the furnace.

The last of ten charges of charcoal went into the furnace at ten o'clock at night, but still the bellows-pumping continued for over an hour before Ron capped off the blowing hole and everyone went to bed. During the day, Ron had used a total of 10 kilos (20lb) of ore and 20 kilos (40lb) of charcoal and people had been constantly working the bellows for 12 hours. But still Ron did not know whether he had succeeded in producing a bloom. 'We were soaking wet but we'd had a damn good day. When I went to bed that night, I couldn't sleep – not because I was cold, but because I couldn't get the smelting out of my mind.'

The following day, the furnace was still very hot, but Ron was able to dig out the slag and cinders. By gently prodding the lower part of the furnace with an iron bar, he knew that a large, dark lump was stuck to the side, about three-quarters of the way down from the top. His hopes were raised. 'I was much more confident at that stage. I knew there was something down there, but it was so hot we couldn't look down the furnace, so we couldn't see what it was.' By gently tapping the lump, he was able to hear what sounded like the distinct ring of metal on metal. Delighted, he now rated his chances of success at better than 90 per cent. But he had to wait to allow the 'lump' to cool down even more before it could be removed. 'I had to hold off because I knew it would still be too hot and fragile and I didn't want to damage it. It was absolute murder having to wait for it to cool.'

Iron Age tools

The Iron Age period is defined by the metal that revolutionized man's ability to exploit his natural resources. Yet the transition from a bronze- to an iron-based culture took more than a thousand years, so the change is perhaps better defined as evolutionary rather than revolutionary. Even during the Iron Age, bronze still had many uses, especially for personal items or pieces of a highly decorative nature.

No self-respecting high status Iron Age Briton would be without their personal knife. Just as the mobile phone has become the essential personal accessory in the early twenty-first century, so a short, well-honed knife was an indispensable accessory in the third century BC. A typical knife would be 15 to 20cm (6 to 8in) long with a handle made of wood, bone or antler and a sharp,

△ A diverse selection of Iron Age tools, including a fish-hook, an axe-head and two spearheads.

carbonized blade. It would be used for everything from eating to carving, and perhaps even a little self-defence. Lower status Celts probably made do with wood, bone or antler knives.

Iron Age men probably shaved with a flat bronze razor, held in the palm of their hand (see page 67). The blade had to be constantly sharpened to keep a fine edge and the action must have been more of scraping than cutting. Other household 'tools' would have included hair combs made from bone, and sewing needles of iron, bronze, bone or antler. Very high-status women might have used a highly polished bronze mirror, but most people would have made do with their reflection in a bucket of water.

Iron woodworking tools were a great improvement over bronze. The Iron Age carpenter would use a wide range of tools, including an adze, side axes, saws, billhooks, files, hammers, awls and gouges.

The use of iron also allowed advances to be made in agricultural tools. The sharp point of an ard could be reinforced with an iron shoe and these are sometimes found in archaeological sites, even though the rest of the wooden implement has long since decayed.

Hand digging and mining were often accomplished with nothing more than an antler pick, although wooden shovels might have been used to move loose material. The back-breaking jobs of haymaking and harvesting were only interrupted by the need to constantly re-sharpen the various sickles and cutting tools used by the labourers.

▷ Ron's bellows were of a modern design rather than strictly Iron Age, but they worked well – at least until they caught fire!

||

Blacksmiths' tools have changed very little since the Iron Age – the smith remains the only craftsman who is capable of making his own tools. These include long-handled tongs, hammers, files, stone and iron anvils and, of course, leather bellows.

△ Bethan uses an antler pick to dig a pit for a bonfire clamp to fire the first batch of pots. The antler pick was used in both farming and mining as early as the Neolithic period.

▷ Ron had a wide selection of traditional Iron Age equipment for use in the forge, although modern tools (such as the hammer in the foreground) mysteriously found their way into his collection!

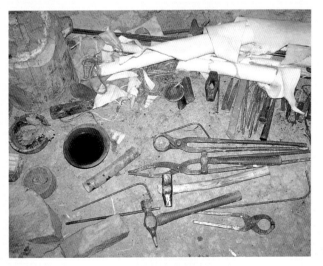

▽ Ron with his successful iron bloom. It took two attempts and about twelve hours to smelt a bucket of iron ore to this stage. It would take several more hours to forge the bloom into a small nugget of iron.

The following morning, the Serpentae gathered by the forge to watch Ron and Brenda retrieve the lump from the furnace. 'That morning, I was never so nervous in all my life, with all the people and the cameras around,' Ron recalls. 'I didn't want to go mad and spoil it.' After gentle persuasion, he removed a piece of bloom not much bigger than a man's fist. The solid mass of iron had not melted, but had undergone physical and chemical changes to leave a dense, spongy mass of metal and impurities. Ron and Brenda had succeeded in producing an iron bloom – the first stage of iron-making on which 600 years of Celtic culture was based.

The next stage is to remove the impurities in the bloom by repeated heating and hammering until the last of the slag is gone. This is a difficult stage because the bloom is brittle and can easily shatter when struck. The process takes even more time, energy and fuel. Ron estimated that it had already taken nearly 60 hours of labour to obtain his bloom, including making the charcoal and smelting the ore. At the end of the process, his bloom was reduced to a piece of iron no bigger than a golf ball.

During the Iron Age, it would take several iron blooms to make an iron ingot of useful size. By the second century BC, the shape of these ingots had become standardized in the form of a long flat bar similar in size and shape to a sword, but with turned-up ends. Julius Caesar remarked that the Britons traded with these iron bars, which subsequently became known as currency bars. Each bar weighed around half a kilo (1lb) and could be used to produce several small tools.

The volunteers spent the last few days on the hillfort preparing for Samhain. Of all the festivals in the Celtic calendar, Samhain was the most important – and the most disturbing. It was celebrated on the evening of 31 October and throughout the following day. This was the night, they believed, when the veil between the living and the spirit world was at its most transparent and when ancestors could return to commune with the living. Samhain was therefore also a festival of the dead, and by all accounts it must have been a fearful time for the early Celts when the spirits from the 'otherworld' had to be placated by those who were still alive.

The volunteers had planned well ahead for their final night on the hillfort. They had brewed honey cider well in advance, baked honey-sweetened oatcakes and were patiently spit-roasting the Dexter steer over an open fire. But their biggest achievement of all was the completion of the wicker man, probably the single most famous symbol of the Iron Age. If the reports of the classical writers are true, then the

THE WICKER MAN

The burning of the wicker man – a huge effigy made from branches and reeds – was one of the most terrifying sacrificial rituals of the Iron Age.

You must build your own wicker man as part of your celebration of Samhain – your final night in the Iron Age. Prepare to erect the statue on the morning of your celebration.

Your wicker man must be at least 20 feet tall and filled with straw. Think also about what else you might wish to pack into the structure.

▽ Hoisting the wicker man into position on their final afternoon.
Unlike their Celtic ancestors, the volunteers decided *not* to fill
the body of the effigy with human and animal sacrifices.

burning of a wicker man must have been one of the more feared and gruesome of the Celtic sacrificial rites. The Greek historian Strabo wrote about the practice: '… having devised a colossus of straw and wood, [they] throw into the colossus cattle and wild animals of all sorts and human beings, and then make a burnt-offering of the whole thing … They offered their sacrifices not without a druid …'

THE CELTIC FESTIVALS

The Irish texts suggest that the Celts celebrated four main festivals during the year. As well as placating the gods, these marked the passage of the seasons and offered a welcome break from the relentless drudgery in the fields. Many of these festivals were shrewdly absorbed by the early monks into the Christian calendar and we still celebrate most of them today. The ancient Celts calculated a day as starting from sunset and not at midnight as we do today, so the eve of a feast day was part of the celebration as well.

The Celtic year started in late autumn, so Samhain was the first and most important festival of the year. It marked the end of summer and the beginning of winter and celebrated the passing of the old year and the beginning of the new. It was thus a time which belonged to neither one year nor the other and the world could therefore be overrun by the forces of magic. The superstitious Celts believed their long-dead ancestors could return during Samhain and the festival found its way into the Christian calendar as All Souls' Day, more commercially known now as Hallowe'en.

Imbolc was celebrated in early February and was probably associated with the lactation of ewes during the lambing season. The festival is now celebrated in the Christian calendar as Candlemas, which falls roughly forty days after Christmas. This is also the feast day of St Brigid, the patron saint of childbirth. Imbolc was probably associated with fertility and was seen as an appropriate time for a new beginning and for re-dedications.

Beltane (or Beltain), the 'fire of Belinos', was celebrated on the first day of May and was an opportunity to celebrate the warmth of the sun and the coming of summer. It has been assimilated into the modern calendar as May Day, traditionally associated with the maypole fertility dance. Beltane was the time of year when the cattle were taken out into open grazing. One of the Celtic rituals was to drive animals, especially cows, between two fires. This ritual probably represented a form of purification before the fertile period of summer.

Finally, the festival of Lughnasa was held in early August to coincide with the ripening of crops and the beginning of the harvest. The festival celebrated the long days of summer and a plentiful supply of food and it was almost certainly a time of great celebration and feasting.

Julius Caesar even suggested that the custom was used as a punishment for petty crime. '[They] use figures of immense size, whose limbs, woven out of twigs, they fill with living men and set on fire … They believe that the execution of those who have been caught in the act of theft or robbery or some crime is more pleasing to the immortal gods; but when the supply of such fails they resort to the execution even of the innocent.'

Shortly before dusk, Chris led the volunteers down the hill carrying their own wicker man which they hauled into an upright position in the middle of a small field. Emma was amazed at what they had built. 'It was the climax of everything that we had worked towards and I was really surprised at what it looked like. I had no idea what to expect because I didn't know what a wicker man was meant to be like. When we pulled it up, it looked so amazing.'

The hazel and cane figure was stuffed with straw and hay and each of the volunteers placed inside the body something which was meaningful to their stay on the hillfort. Chris left a wooden whistle which he had made in memory of the music and song they had enjoyed together, and Ceris her waterproof cape which she would no longer need in the modern world. Brenda carefully inserted her calendar slate, on which she had faithfully recorded the passing days since their arrival. Ron donated kale (which he never wanted ever to eat again) and Emma a steak from the steer they had slaughtered. Anne bundled some wool together to represent the jumble of ideas and thoughts that were rushing through her head.

As the sun set over the Preseli Hills, the Serpentae lit their torches made from wood, hay and sheep fat and walked in procession down the hill towards their effigy, chanting, 'Burn him, burn him,' as they went. In preparation for the festival, Ceris used blue woad and her artistic talents to good effect. 'I painted everybody's face … I did more on Anne's face because she was the chief and I drew a swirl on her cheek and bits under her eyes.'

For Emma, life in the Iron Age suddenly took on a real meaning. 'When we lit the wicker man, it was so warm and the evening was pure fun. I began to realize what the Celts must have felt like. Theirs was a life of extremes. They would have worked hard and worried about eating enough, then they would really enjoy themselves and eat whole steers and have lots of fun. It felt really decadent. It was sheer abandonment.'

Like the rest of the group, Ron Phillips was also determined to make the most of their last evening together. 'I bloody loved it. I really got into everything. It was a

THE CELTIC WAY OF DEATH

From the end of the Bronze Age through to the early Iron Age, the disposal of the dead left very little archaeological evidence. Some remains, however, have been found within the confines of a settlement, often buried in a storage pit. At the Danebury hillfort for example, 300 separate finds of human remains have been recovered from pits, but only 38 comprise more or less complete bodies; the rest vary from odd bones and skulls to partial skeletons. This suggests that there was little respect shown to bodies after death, although this could also reflect their unfree status.

What happened to the vast majority of the early Iron Age people at the time of death remains a mystery. The dead might have been cremated, the bodies might have been left exposed until the flesh was gone before scattering or destroying the bones, or perhaps a form of 'sky-burial' was used similar to the rituals adopted by Tibetans today.

By the fourth century BC (roughly the middle of the Iron Age), however, there is evidence that the rituals surrounding death had begun to change. Mid-Iron Age cemeteries have been excavated at Deal in Kent and in East Yorkshire. In both cases, the bodies had been treated with dignity and buried intact (unlike the Danebury bodies), although coffins were not used. In Yorkshire, the extensive cemeteries of the 'Arras Culture' (named after the first excavation just outside the town of Market Weighton) contain as many as 500 graves laid out within a clearly defined compound.

In both regions, the cemeteries contain the remains of adults of both sexes and more than half of the burials are devoid of any grave goods which might indicate status. However, those inhumations which do contain grave offerings include those of high status men and women who were buried with chariots; the men were usually buried with swords and armour, while the women were accompanied by iron mirrors. One woman, presumably a leader, was found in the Wetwang Slack cemetery in a grave laid out with the bodies of armed male warriors alongside her.

Lower down the hierarchy were individual male warriors who were buried with swords; the youngest was approximately 17 years old and the oldest in his mid-forties. In some instances in the Yorkshire cemeteries, spears were thrust into a shield which covered the corpse, and sometimes directly into the body itself, after it was laid to rest in the grave. This might have been part of a ceremony celebrating a warrior hero.

Early in the first century BC, the practice of cremation was introduced to southern Britain from the continent and burials were often accompanied by drinking and feasting, much like an Irish wake today. In the 'Welwyn Burials' of the mid to late first century BC, wealthy men were cremated and their ashes interred with silver, bronze, glass and ceramic drinking vessels, together with amphorae which originally contained 26 litres (35 standard bottles) of wine imported from Italy.

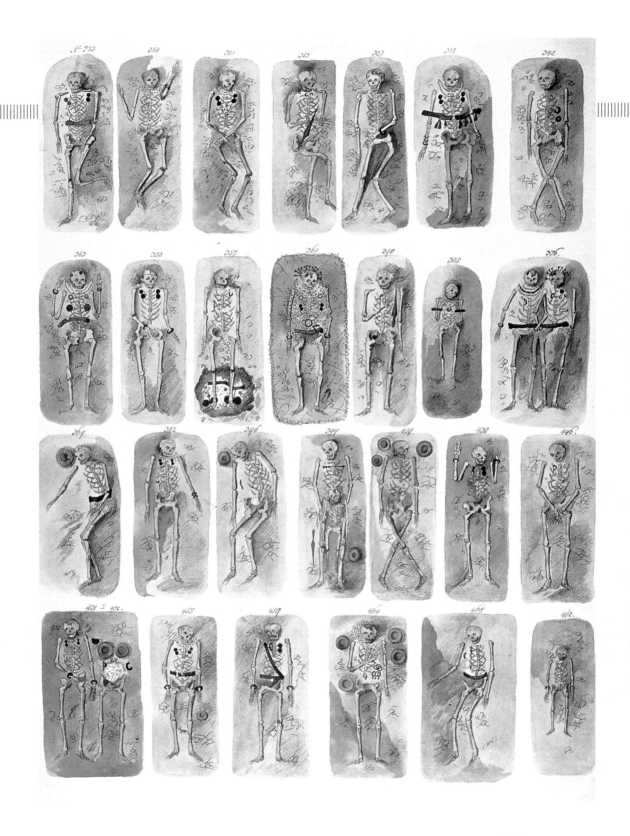

super end to the weeks we'd had there. It is something I'll always remember every year on that day. It was fantastic. We all had a damn good time.'

The volunteers had a slow start the next day. Their few belongings still needed to be packed and goodbyes said to the geese. Those who were not suffering a hangover from the night before toasted the ancient Celts in champagne, knowing full well that whatever life they were going back to in the twenty-first century, it would not be as physically demanding as the one they were leaving behind.

Chris held a short closing ceremony around the fire in the chieftain's house. Mark gathered up ash from their communal fire and everybody was given some to take home with them, to add to their fire at home as a continuation of the spirit of community and friendship which had developed among these twelve people. A little more than six weeks previously they had come together as strangers. They had experienced laughter and tears together, success and failure, illness and health. They would never have met at all had it not been for the chance opportunity of living in the Iron Age. Now they left as friends.

Like all the volunteers, Bethan felt a great sense of achievement but it was mixed with trepidation about going home. 'I knew I would miss the freedom of the place. I was also apprehensive about trying to tell my friends what it was like – they would never understand what we'd been through.' Tom too was in a reflective mood. 'I'm really having a good time. Although I'm looking forward to going home, I would be happy to stay here for a bit longer. I'm beginning to realize how Mum and Dad coped with it for a year. After the initial shock of the first month, it's become so much easier to survive – no one's been ill and the food is OK.' Jody too would have stayed

▽ Their last morning at Castell Henllys and a toast to the Iron Age. After seven weeks isolated from the modern world, Tom marvelled at the perfect form of a champagne glass.

longer. 'I'm comfortable, I don't mind getting a bit wet and muddy. I just really, really love it here and I don't want it to end.'

The group left the same way as they had arrived, on foot and carrying their few possessions. They stopped briefly at the sacred spring for a final goodbye. Then they walked on down the hill, past the stream and on to the medieval church at Meline, where they boarded the coach that would take them back to the twenty-first century.

That evening at the hotel, the volunteers met for a thank-you party with the small army of local people who had helped to support them during their stay at the hillfort. To mark the occasion, Dave Rickard kept everyone amused with a folk song which he had written, sung to the tune of *I'll be a Wild Rover*:

WILD ROVING CELTS

As Iron Age people on a hillfort in Wales,
  We lasted six weeks eating lamb, wheat and kale.
The buckets were leaky, the shoes they all split,
  We ate dodgy chicken which gave us the … runs!

    And it's no, nay, never,
    No nay never no more ,
    Will we stay on that hillfort,
    No never, no more.

We had to make charcoal and brew honey beer,
  Make serpents and baskets and all kinds of gear.
We had to bloom iron and fish in the rain,
  And the film crew said, 'Great – can you do it again?'

    And it's no, nay, never,
    No nay never no more ,
    Will we stay on that hillfort,
    No never, no more.

We had windy old houses and lumpy old beds,
  And the wind whistling round blew the hair off Ron's head.
But now we're returning to the warmth of the light,
  And we'll have a great time at the party tonight.

    And it's no, nay, never,
    No nay never no more ,
    Will we stay on that hillfort,
    No never, no more.

◁ Throughout their seven weeks on the hillfort, the volunteers were constantly under the scrutiny of the video crew: Darren Tate (far left) on sound and Rob Llewellyn on camera.

▽ The twelve who really did survive: (back left) Dave, Mark, Ceris and Tom; (centre) Brenda, Ron, Anne and Jody; (bottom) Bethan, little Chris, Emma and big Chris.

12
Back to the Future

FOR MOST OF THE VOLUNTEERS, their return to the modern world was a culture shock every bit as profound as the one they experienced when they moved into the hillfort. Everybody commented on the bright colours, the noise and the frenetic pace of the present-day world. Tom remembers that everything was 'in your face', although he and Ceris did go clubbing on their first night home, so it is little wonder that he found the experience a shock. Emma sat up all night watching pop videos, transfixed by the music, the colour and the action. Ron too was struck by television. 'Colour was so vivid. The TV especially was so bright and vivid. It hit me like a tonne of bricks – the colour was fabulous.'

Despite enjoying the obvious luxuries of the modern world, such as the warmth of centrally heated houses, comfortable beds and hot baths, nobody found the transition back to the twenty-first century easy to make. Emma found it every bit as difficult as moving into the Iron Age. 'My whole attitude to dirt has changed. I've been back three weeks now and I haven't bothered to clean my house.' Chris Park in particular found it difficult to settle and within a couple of weeks he was back in Pembrokeshire, this time building stone circles with friends near the Iron Age fort of Carningli, no more than a few miles from Castell Henllys. He too missed the simplicity of life in the Iron Age and would quite happily have stayed in the fort for a much longer period.

Ron was taken aback by how rude and aggressive people were on the street and Brenda wanted to go back to the fort, where she found life simple, peaceful and hassle-free. Jody too remarked on people's behaviour. 'Everybody always seems to be in a bad mood. I went to Tesco's and everybody was jostling each other and giving each other bad looks. It was so different in the community.'

In general, they all felt they were more relaxed after the project and thought the experience had given them a fresh perspective on life. Jody believed her time in the Iron Age had completely changed her outlook; she felt she was a calmer person

▽ The volunteers enjoy their first meal back in the twenty-first century. As a special treat, the BBC asked the hotel to prepare a rare and delicious dish for them – boiled kale!

and found it easier to keep things in balance. Ron and Brenda also thought that life had changed for the better and they were able to see things in a much simpler way. As Ron commented, 'Life's going to be a lot steadier, a whole lot brighter and a lot more fun!' Bethan remembers reading a women's magazine at the hotel and being shocked at some of the articles and the superficial importance of looking good. 'On the hillfort, nobody knew what they looked like and we really didn't care. The individual was the most important thing.' Jody too felt liberated by the experience and had learnt not to judge others by their appearance.

Having to deal with money was another issue which kept cropping up in conversations with the volunteers. Emma went out on the first weekend and bought £60 worth of cosmetics she did not need. The money meant nothing to her; it was the simple act of spending money which she found exciting and which gave her power and status. Ron and Brenda too were fascinated by their ability to stop and buy things whenever they wanted and marvelled at the range and diversity of goods on the shelves. Tom commented on how flawless articles seemed to be in the modern world, and he remembers marvelling at the perfect form of a champagne glass. For some reason, he also found it difficult getting used to chairs with backs.

Bethan, however, had lost all interest in possessions and quite happily walked past clothes shops without a second glance. On her first Sunday back, her church was running an appeal and she found herself giving away many of the belongings which previously had been important to her. In fact, her mother had to stop her giving away half the household possessions!

All the volunteers remarked on how important friendship had become. They had missed their friends and family from home, but they had also developed a close bond together on the hillfort. Bethan remarked on how she had become used to always having somebody around and once they had left the site, she experienced a sense of loss and loneliness. Mark too was very aware of the importance of the friendships that had developed over the previous weeks. 'I think everyone will miss each other because we've really built up quite strong bonds, strong friendships. So it will be really strange not seeing any of the faces that I'm used to now. Obviously, spending seven weeks not being able to get away from them and being friends with them – you can't then just go the rest of your life without seeing them.'

THE END OF THE IRON AGE

During the last two centuries BC, the expanding Roman Empire gradually subdued the Iron Age societies of Europe. As Rome began to control more of the continent, so trading patterns began to shift as entrepreneurs exploited new opportunities.

Hengistbury Head, overlooking Christchurch harbour in Dorset, was Britain's most important port during the late Iron Age. Here, imported luxury goods such as Italian wine, Breton pottery and raw glass were moved inland up the rivers Stour and Avon. In return, items such as slaves, hides, metal and hunting dogs were exported to the continent. There was such a high demand for slaves in Rome that slave-trading in late Iron Age Britain may well have had a disruptive effect on society similar to that which the American slave trade had on West Africa in more recent times, and this might have hastened the eventual decline of Iron Age Britain.

Once Julius Caesar succeeded in his conquest of Gaul (58–51 BC), trade along the Atlantic seaboard declined in favour of inland waterways in France and Germany. Consequently the port at Hengistbury Head fell into decline after about 50 BC as Roman trade with Britain moved to East Anglia. As new trading centres grew up in Essex and Hertfordshire, the wealth and importance of Wessex and western England declined.

Iron Age Britain progressively became more closely linked to Rome and when the Romans landed in Kent in AD 43, they began their conquest of Britain in earnest. It was to take them over 40 years, but this proved to be the death knell of Iron Age society in Britain.

Resistance to the Roman invaders varied between the different Iron Age tribes. The Atrebates of central southern England offered little resistance and might even have become allies from the beginning. The Durotriges, however, were made of sterner stuff and their opposition was ruthlessly suppressed by the Romans. Queen Boudica rallied support amongst several tribes in AD 60–61 and successfully mounted a rebellion in eastern England, but even her success was short-lived.

Within a few generations, the face of lowland Britain was dramatically changed by Roman occupation. Paved roads criss-crossed the country, towns were established and stone villas, some of them palatial, were scattered throughout the country. The Romans eventually occupied an area of Britain which roughly equates to present-day England and Wales, but they were less successful in Scotland.

The eventual collapse of the Roman Empire in the fifth century AD proved to be a disaster for the native Britons. The departing Romans left a power vacuum which was filled by the Angles and Saxons, who moved in from the Low Countries and settled in the east of the country. The invaders eventually established a Germanic-speaking England and forced the native Celts ever more westwards, towards the West Country and Wales.

Looking back, illness from infected food had been a problem for many of the volunteers, especially in the early weeks. Bill, Anne and David probably caught salmonella from eating partially cooked chicken in the first few days, and little Rosie was diagnosed with campylobacter in the second week. In fact, these illnesses are generally much more common today than they were even a decade ago. This has led some medical experts to wonder if we are not making our world over-sanitized. It is possible that our immune systems no longer have routine skirmishes with infections to keep them robust and effective. This concept has been called the 'hygiene hypothesis' and some doctors now think that because we are exposed less and less to general infection, our immune systems are not ready to fight back when needed. It is interesting to note that during the first Iron Age project twenty-three years previously, there was virtually no illness amongst the people over a whole year.

The other big problem the volunteers had faced in the early days was a lack of strength and stamina. It was not until the water tap was relocated at the top of the hill and firewood was brought up to the site that they had found the time and the energy to tackle their 'time challenges'. Anne especially found the Iron Age lifestyle hard work. 'I think we were physically exhausted because we simply didn't have the strength of the Iron Age people. We had twenty-first century strength, and we just had to build up to it.'

Professor Barry Cunliffe is one of the country's leading Iron Age archaeologists. When he visited the project during the Cantiaci week-end, he remarked how physically demanding life must have been during the period. 'There's no doubt that the amount of physical work needed at certain times of the year just to stay alive was far, far more than we can anticipate. Just going down to get the water from the nearby spring would have been perfectly normal for most Iron Age societies. Here it's not terribly far away, but at one of the sites I excavated in Hampshire at Danebury hillfort, water was about a kilometre or a kilometre and a half away, and every day

△ Professor Barry Cunliffe from Oxford University was a consultant for both BBC Iron Age series.

people would have had to go down and bring water up. The maintenance of the fields with primitive tools, looking after the flocks, bringing in the hay – all of these things would have been colossally labour-intensive.'

Despite the physical hardship and the restricted diet, everyone remarked how much healthier they felt. On average, all the older people had lost around 7 kilos (15lb) in body weight. Anne remarked that Dave was positively running around the house when they got back, with much more energy than normal. Ron too thought he was much fitter than he had been for years, but he did notice that his chronic catarrh, which had disappeared completely during his time at the fort, returned once he moved back into a centrally heated house.

The volunteers had also derived great satisfaction from learning new skills and taking on their 'time challenges'. Dave Rickard even went so far as to make his own oven cleaner once he was home, by mixing a little detergent with wood ash and working it into a thick paste. He declared it to be very effective. Ron and Brenda were especially thrilled to have succeeded with the iron smelting and thought it was the achievement of a lifetime. Their shaft furnace is now going to be left to deteriorate so that archaeologists can record how it disintegrates over time, and this could help them to interpret the remains of Iron Age furnaces.

The BBC project was always intended to be about how twenty-first century people coped with living under prehistoric conditions and there was never any expectation that we would learn much about how the Iron Age people actually lived. However, Professor Barry Cunliffe found that he began to look at the Iron Age through fresh eyes. 'The sort of thing that I am learning is people's different concept of time. Yesterday I was watching people moving about the place. They were moving slowly and fairly purposefully, but not in a busy way. All of their sense of time was different …

'I was talking to the blacksmith in the house that was used as his forge. There was a girl there working the bellows and it was the most beautiful, quite relaxing time. This must have affected the minds of the people and the way they responded to nature, the way they responded to each other, the way they responded to their own creative abilities.

'Now, none of this you can get by being an archaeologist, no matter how good you are. You've got to experience all these intangible things, and that opens up the mind. It makes you think very differently … That's the sort of thing I get out of an experience like this.'

Dave Rickard, on the other hand, thought that his experience of living in the Iron Age gave him an insight into how life should be lived in the twenty-first century. 'One thing that the project has brought to my mind is the whole question of ecology and the balance of nature. Nature has its own cycles – there's no such thing as waste in nature, everything is used, everything is a resource. When something dies, it becomes food for something else, and the whole cycle repeats itself.

'The Iron Age people must have been pretty close to that. They would have had a fairly hard life in many respects. There wouldn't have been much in the way of luxuries and certainly not enough to throw away. If there was a surplus of something, they would have found a way of keeping it to use later. The project made me realize how much twenty-first century people are into packaged goods and junk and things like that. So this experience will only have hardened my resolve to keep as far away from that sort of thing as I can when I get back home.'

Appendix 1
Equipping the Iron Age Project

ACCOMMODATION

Chieftain's roundhouse, sleeps 6
Middle roundhouse, sleeps 6 to 10
Lower roundhouse/store house, sleeps 7
Small roundhouse/forge, sleeps 1 to 2
Four-post granary
Hen house

PERSONAL POSSESSIONS

Wooden bowls, cups and plates (55)
Wooden spoons and knives (100)
Wooden containers and bowls (30)
Iron knives (10)
Bone knives (10)
Bronze razors (2)
Bronze mirror (1)
Bone combs and needles, bronze needles
    and pins (25)
Four-poster wooden beds (6)
Hurdle beds (11)
Hay mattresses (17)
Woollen rugs (45)
Blankets (15)
Wooden chests with emergency equipment
    (including fire extinguishers,
    emergency torches, first aid kit and
    emergency mobile phone) (4)

HOUSEHOLD & COMMUNAL GOODS

Rotary querns (3)
Saddle quern (1)
Wooden spit roast (1)
Copper cauldron (1)

Iron cauldrons (5)
Cauldron chains (4)
Griddle plates (4)
Chains and hooks for hams
Large baskets (50)
Very large baskets with lids (4)
Lining for baskets (10)
Wooden buckets (16)
Large wooden tubs (3)
Wooden barrels (3)
Bread ovens (3)
Shelves for ovens (2)
Hot griddle-iron flat plates (2)
Candles (20% to be beeswax) (200)
Benches (3 in each main house)
Outside benches (5)
Wattle partitions for houses (12)
Chopping boards, various sizes (10)

GENERAL SITE SUPPLIES

Hazel bundles (130)
Willow bundles (24)
Wattle palisade and fences
Palisade posts (22)
Refurbishment of granary and hen house
New latrine
Hollow wooden trough (1)
Outdoor benches (5)
Hay bales (10)
Daub
Leather hides (50)
Tanned cow hide (4)
Woollen fleeces (40)

SPECIALIST EQUIPMENT & TOOLS

Stone anvil (1)
Tongs (4)
Axes (3)
Adze (1)
Hammers (5)
Saws (2)
Chisels (4)
Gouges (2)
Bill hooks (3)
Files (5)
Currency bars (5)
Bellows (1)
Hemp rope and twine
    (various sizes up to 12mm)
Fish and eel traps (6)
Shields (3)
Wooden spades (2)
Pole lathe (1)
Wooden ard (1)
Wooden sled (1)
One small and one large ladder
Weaving looms (2)
Loom weights (48)
Spindles and whorls (10)
Antler picks (4)
Slings and shot (10)
Loom and wool
Antler bones (10)
Bone (15)
Cow horn (20)
Updraught pottery kiln

FOOD

Rams for slaughter (5)
Dexter steer for slaughter (1)
Chickens for eggs and eating (24)
Geese (2)
Various hams and cheeses
Spelt wheat for grinding
Flour and bread
Kale
Apples
Honey
Dried herbs
Fresh planted herbs
Honey beer (40 gallons)

PERSONAL CLOTHING

Men & boys
Medium tunic
Long linen tunic
Medium linen tunic
Braecci or long trousers
Woollen cloak
Leather shoes
Belt and brooch

Women & girls
Long gown
Full-length skirt
Medium tunic
Long tunic
Long linen tunic
Medium linen tunic
Woollen cloak
Leather shoes
Belt and brooch

APPENDIX 2

Places to visit: Iron Age sites, websites and museums

The British Isles still retain a wealth of Iron Age sites which are well worth a visit. The main sites are marked on the Ordnance Survey 1:50,000 scale maps, the OS Map of Southern Britain in the Iron Age and on many commercial road maps.

England
Rough Tor and Tregeare Rounds, Cornwall
Maiden Castle, Hengistbury Head and Bindon Hill, Dorset
South Cadbury and Badbury Ring, Somerset
Bathhampton Down, Somerset
Danebury, Beacon Hill and Balkesbury, Hampshire
Uffington Castle and the White Horse, Berkshire
Winklebury, Wiltshire
Hartington Beacon, Sussex
Midsummer Hill, British Camp and Hereford Beacon, Hereford and Worcester
Almondbury and Ingleborough, Yorkshire

Wales
Castell Henllys hillfort, Bosherston promontory fort and St David's Head, Pembrokeshire
Caerau hillfort, near Cardiff, South Wales
Pen Dinas, near Aberystwyth, Ceredigion
Tre'r Ceiri, Gwynedd

Scotland
The Caterthuns and Finavon, Angus
Dun Telve and Dun Troddan Brochs, Glenelg, Highlands
Dun Ardtreck Broch, Isle of Skye
Midhowe, Aikerness and Gueress Brochs, Orkney Islands
Clickhimin, Ness of Burgi and Broch of Mousa, Shetland Islands

For a comprehensive index of ancient sites in Europe, try
   http://easyweb.easynet.co.uk/~aburnham/database/geog_idx.htm

RECONSTRUCTED IRON AGE ROUNDHOUSES AND SETTLEMENTS

BUTSER ANCIENT FARM is a replica of an Iron Age farmstead c.300 BC and includes buildings, animals and crops of the kind that existed at that time. Open to the public and school parties. Situated four miles south of Petersfield in Hampshire, just off the A3. *Telephone* 023 92 598 838. http://www.skcldv.demon.co.uk/iafintro.htm

THE CANTIACI LIVING HISTORY GROUP have a typical late Iron Age farmstead and roundhouse on display at the Riverside Country Park in Gillingham, Kent. Open all year by appointment. *Telephone* 01634 378987. http://www.cantiaci.co.uk/

CASTELL HENLLYS is open to the public from Easter to the end of October and to school parties all year. The hillfort lies off the A487 in Pembrokeshire, about four miles east of Newport. *Telephone* 01239 891319. http://castellhenllys.pembrokeshirecoast.org.uk/

MICHELHAM PRIORY at Upper Dicker, near Hailsham, East Sussex has a roundhouse on display, modelled on the dwellings excavated at the hillfort at Hollingbury, north of Brighton. Open from mid-March to the end of October. *Telephone* 01323 844224. http://www.sussexpast.co.uk/mich/rhouse.htm

THE MUSEUM OF WELSH LIFE at St Fagans near Cardiff has an Iron Age village with roundhouses and an iron-making furnace. It is signposted from junction 33 on the M4 motorway, about four miles west of Cardiff. Open all year. *Telephone* 029 2057 3500. http://www.nmgw.ac.uk/mwl/index.en.shtml

THE ANCIENT TECHNOLOGY CENTRE in Dorset has five roundhouses as well as other structures. Offering opportunities for experimental archaeology, it welcomes school parties and visitors by appointment. *Telephone* 01725 517618. http://www.dorset-lea.org.uk/atc

THE NEW BARN FIELD CENTRE in Dorset has a Celtic village and other attractions. It can be found 2 miles north-west of Dorchester, off the A37. Open 10 a.m. every day from Easter to the end of September. *Telephone* 01305 268856. http://www.newbarn.co.uk/

THE PEAT MOORS CONSERVATION CENTRE at Westhay near Glastonbury has an Iron Age settlement and wooden trackways on display. Open April to October, 10 a.m. to 5 p.m. *Telephone* 01458 860697. http://somerset.gov.uk/levels/pmvc.htm

MUSEUMS

THE BRITISH MUSEUM
Great Russell Street, London WC1B 3DG
Telephone 020 7323 8000. http://www.thebritishmuseum.ac.uk/

THE NATIONAL MUSEUM OF WALES
Cathays Park, Cardiff CF10 3NP
Telephone 029 2039 7951. http://www.nmgw.ac.uk/

THE MUSEUM OF SCOTLAND
Chambers Street, Edinburgh EH1 1JF
Telephone 0131 225 7534. http://www.nms.ac.uk/

THE MUSEUM OF THE IRON AGE (for Danebury artefacts)
Church Street, Andover, Hampshire SP10 1DP
Telephone 01264 366283. http://www.hants.gov.uk/museum/ironagem/

THE DORSET COUNTY MUSEUM (for Maiden Castle artefacts)
High West Street, Dorchester, Dorset DT1 1XA
Telephone 01305 262735. http://home.clara.net/dorset.museum/

THE ASHMOLEAN MUSEUM
Beaumont Street, Oxford OX1 2PH
Telephone 01865 278000. http://www.ashmol.ox.ac.uk/

THE YORKSHIRE MUSEUM
Museum Gardens, York YO1 7FR
Telephone 01904 551800. http://www.york.gov.uk/heritage/museums/yorkshire/

HULL AND EAST RIDING MUSEUM (for Arras artefacts)
36 High Street, Hull HU1 1PS
Telephone 01482 613902. http://www.hullcc.gov.uk/museums/hullandeastriding.html

IPSWICH MUSEUM & ART GALLERY
High Street, Ipswich, Suffolk IP1 3QH
Telephone 01473 433550. http://www.ipswich.gov.uk/tourism/guide/museum.htm

COLCHESTER CASTLE MUSEUM (for Roman garrison)
Castle Park, High Street, Colchester, Essex CO1 1TJ
Telephone 01206 282939. http://www.colchester.gov.uk/leisure/seedo/musindx.htm

USEFUL WEBSITES

BBC ONLINE has a website with further details of the Iron Age project:
http://www.bbc.co.uk/history/

THE UNIVERSITY OF YORK'S DEPT OF ARCHAEOLOGY has detailed information of their
excavation at Castell Henllys: http://www.york.ac.uk/depts/arch/staff/sites/henllys/menu.htm

THE WORLD OF THE CELTS
http://www.gallica.co.uk/

CURRENT ARCHAEOLOGY
http://www.archaeology.co.uk/

Glossary

adze A wood cutting tool shaped like an axe but with the blade at right angles to the haft.

amphora A ceramic container used to carry oil or wine from the Mediterranean.

ard A simple type of Iron Age plough which breaks the soil but does not turn it.

Arras culture An Iron Age culture based on burial tradition and grave goods, which occupied an area of East Yorkshire from the fifth to first centuries BC.

barrow A prehistoric burial mound.

Beltane An early Celtic festival celebrated at the beginning of May and associated with the beginning of summer and the purification of cows. (Also spelt Beltain).

braecci Long trousers.

Bronze Age The middle age of the three prehistoric periods, during which bronze was the main metal used for tools and weapons. In Britain, the Bronze Age lasted from approximately 2500 to 650 BC.

causewayed camp A Neolithic community gathering site used for social events and sometimes death rituals.

Celts The name given to prehistoric Iron Age tribes in Europe who shared similar traditions. The Celts dominated the continent from about 650 BC to the time of the Roman period. The Greeks called them *Keltoí* and the Romans *Celtae*.

Charcoal clamp A mound of cut timber, covered in turf and soil to exclude the air. When fired, the natural wood gases burn and the wood is carbonized, to produce charcoal.

Classical world A collective term given to the Roman, Greek and Etruscan civilizations.

coppice A managed woodland in which trees such as hazel are regularly cut back to encourage the growth of small branches or 'rods'.

daub A plaster made from clay mixed with various other components including straw, cow manure, soil and sometimes animal hair and blood. Used to plaster wattle fences to make a waterproof wall.

dendrochronology A technique which uses the annual growth rings in trees to establish the age of a wooden object.

druids The priests of a pre-Christian Celtic religion practised in Gaul and Britain until the Roman conquest.

farmstead The basic settlement in the Iron Age, populated by the extended family of a farmer.

Gaul Derivation of the Roman name *Gallia*, given to what is now mainly modern day France. The Romans called the Gallic Celts *Galli* or Gauls.

Hallstatt culture A 'type-site' defining late Bronze and early Iron Age artefacts from central Europe, roughly 1200 to 500 BC. Named after a cemetery site in Austria.

henge A Neolithic structure of banks and ditches, probably used for a religious or ceremonial purpose.

hillfort An Iron Age fort with defensive boundaries, usually inhabited by the extended family of a chieftain or noble.

Imbolc A Celtic festival celebrated in early February. Thought to be associated with the lactation of ewes.

inhumation Burial of the dead (as opposed to cremation).

Iron Age The last phase of prehistory in Europe, following the Bronze Age and preceding the literate Roman era. The Iron Age dates from roughly 650 BC to 50 BC or later, depending on the date of Roman occupation of the area. Iron was the primary metal for the manufacture of tools and weapons during this period.

La Tène culture Like the earlier Hallstatt culture, another 'type-site' which defines the latter part of the Iron Age from about 500 BC.

Lindow Man A well-preserved body of an Iron Age man found in a peat bog in Lindow Moss, just south of Manchester. The man was clearly sacrificed in a ritual manner.

Lughnasa A Celtic festival held at the beginning of August to mark the ripening of crops and the beginning of the harvest.

lynchet A bank which forms in a field as a result of regular ploughing and which gradually moves downhill due to erosion and gravity.

Mesolithic period The middle Stone Age, approximately 8500 to 3500 BC in Britain.

multivallate Defences which comprise more than one bank and ditch.

Neolithic period The cultural period characterized by the first farming communities and the use of polished stone and flint tools and weapons. Also called the new Stone Age, it lasted from approximately 3500 to 2200 BC in Britain.

palisade A wooden fence built around a hillfort or farmstead for defence.

peplum A tubular, sleeveless dress.

quernstone A stone used by Iron Age people for grinding flour; two main designs were used. A rotary quernstone has a top section which rotates over a fixed lower half, whereas a saddle quernstone has a bottom stone shaped like a dish, with a smaller oval stone being used to grind corn in the hollow.

radiocarbon dating A method of dating which measures the amount of radioactive carbon (C-14) remaining in a sample of organic matter.

roundhouse A traditional circular dwelling built from wattle and daub and thatched with straw or reed, inhabited by the Bronze and Iron Age people.

Samhain An Iron Age festival which celebrated the end of the Celtic year. Absorbed into the Christian calendar as All Souls' Day and also celebrated today as Hallowe'en. (Pronounced *Sam-hane*, *Sam-hine* or *Sow-hane.*)

spindle whorls Small discs with a central hole which holds a wooden spindle used to spin wool. They are usually made from stone, clay or bone and are among the most common finds on Iron Age sites.

Stone Age The first of three prehistoric ages when stone and flint were the principle materials used for tools and weapons. See also Mesolithic and Neolithic periods.

torc (or torque) A neck ring of metal, sometimes twisted, worn as jewellery by the Iron Age people. Could be made from iron or bronze (or occasionally silver or gold) and may have been used to denote status.

tumulus See barrow.

tuyere hole A hole in the base of a shaft furnace through which air is blown from a pair of bellows.

votive offering An offering to the gods in fulfilment of a vow or pledge.

wattle A wooden fence or panel made by weaving 'rods' of hazel branches. Extensively used in the Iron Age and often plastered with daub to create a waterproof wall.

wicker man An effigy made from wood and straw, burnt during Iron Age sacrificial rituals. Described by Caesar and other classical writers.

Further Reading

Collis, John, *The European Iron Age* (Batsford, London, 1984)

Chadwick, Nora, *The Celts* (Penguin, London, 1970)

Champion, Timothy et al, *Prehistoric Europe* (Academic Press, London, 1984)

Cunliffe, Barry, *Greeks, Romans and Barbarians* (Batsford, London, 1988)
>   *Iron Age Communities in Britain* (3rd ed.)(Routledge, London, 1991)
>   *Danebury: Anatomy of an Iron Age Hillfort* (Batsford/English Heritage, London, 1993)
>   (ed.) *The Oxford Illustrated Prehistory of Europe* (OUP, Oxford, 1994)
>   *Iron Age Britain* (Batsford/English Heritage, London, 1995)

Delaney, Frank, *The Celts* (Hodder & Stoughton, London, 1986)

Dyer, James, *Hillforts of England and Wales* (2nd rev. ed.)(Shire Archaeology, Princes Risborough, 1992)

Green, M.J., *Celtic Myths* (British Museum Press, London, 1993)
>   (ed.), *The Celtic World* (Routledge, London, 1995)
>   *Exploring the World of the Druids* (Thames & Hudson, London, 1997)
>   *The Gods of the Celts* (Sutton Publishing, Stroud, 1997)

Herdman, M., *Life in Iron Age Britain* (George Harrap, London, 1981)

Hill, David & Jesson, Margaret (ed.),*The Iron Age and its Hill-forts* (Southampton University, Southampton, 1971)

Kruta, V. et al (ed.), *The Celts* (Thames & Hudson, London, 1991)

Laing, Lloyd, *Celtic Britain* (Routledge, London, 1979)

James, Simon, *Exploring the World of the Celts* (Thames & Hudson, London, 1993)
>   *The Atlantic Celts* (British Museum Press, London, 1999)

James, Simon and Rigby, Valery, *Britain and the Celtic Iron Age* (British Museum Press, London, 1997)

Megaw, M.R. and Megaw, J.V.S., *Celtic Art from its Beginnings to the Book of Kells* (Thames & Hudson, London, 1989)

Piggott, Stuart, *The Druids* (Thames & Hudson, London, 1975)

Reynolds, Peter, *Iron-Age Farm* (Colonnade/British Museum, London, 1979)

Rolleston, T.W., *Celtic Myths and Legends* (Senate, London, 1994)

Salway, Peter, *Roman Britain* (Clarendon Press, Oxford, 1981)

Sharples, Niall, *Maiden Castle* (Batsford, London, 1991)

Stead, Ian, *Celtic Art* (British Museum Press, London, 1985)

Index

Picture Credits

AKG London 49, 169; Art Archive 160; BBC 26al, 26ar, 57a, 57b, 58, 59a, 59c, 59b, 69, 76, 84, 109, 124ar, 153r;
BBC Worldwide Ltd/Siân Trenberth 19, 22, 54al, 54ar, 54b, 72al, 72ar, 79a, 79b, 86b, 89r, 104al, 104ar, 108, 154al,
154b, 164, 165, 174b; Bridgeman 42; British Museum 8a, 43, 116, 135a, 135b, 136, 143; Corbis 36al, 36b, 40, 131;
Danebury Trust 18a, 18b, 115; English Heritage 8b; Peter Firstbrook 11, 12a, 12b, 14, 15, 24, 25a, 25b, 26b, 66, 67, 68,
72b, 77, 80, 81, 83, 86al, 86ar, 87, 88, 89l, 91, 92, 93, 95, 97, 98, 101, 104b, 111, 121, 124al, 126, 129, 138b, 141, 144, 146,
147, 149, 153l, 154ar, 156l, 156r, 157, 161l, 161br, 162, 171, 172, 174a, 176, 179; Fortean Picture Library 36ar, 130;
Tom Little 109, 113, 118, 124b, 127, 138a, 150, 161ar; Mary Evans Picture Library 132; Martin Pailthorpe 27, 28, 29,
30, 31, 32, 33, 34, 35, 56